MW00457574

The Leprechaun's Story

AS TOLD BY **LLOYD** TO **TANIS HELLIWELL**

Other books by Tanis Helliwell

Good Morning Henry: an in-depth journey with the body
intelligence

High Beings of Hawaii: encounters with mystical ancestors

Hybrids: so you think you are human

Summer with the Leprechauns: a true story

Pilgrimage with the Leprechauns: a true story of a mystical
tour of Ireland

Decoding Your Destiny: keys to humanity's spiritual
transformation

Manifest Your Soul's Purpose

Embraced by Love: Poems

The Leprechaun's Story

AS TOLD BY **LLOYD** TO
TANIS HELLIWELL

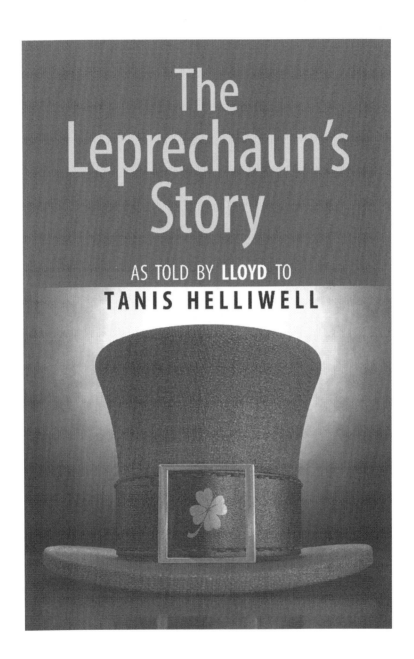

Published by Wayshower Enterprises

Copyright © 2023 by Tanis Helliwell

All rights reserved under International and Pan American Copyright Conventions. No part of this book may be reproduced in any form or by an electronic or mechanical means, including information storage and retrieval systems, without permission in writing from the publisher, except by a reviewer, who may quote brief passages in a review.

Library and Archives Canada Cataloguing in Publication

Title: The leprechaun's story / as recounted by Lloyd to Tanis Helliwell.

Names: Helliwell, Tanis, author.

Description: Includes bibliographical references and index.

Identifiers: Canadiana (print) 20220466300 | Canadiana (ebook) 20220466513
ISBN 9781987831368 (softcover) | ISBN 9781987831382 (Kindle)
ISBN 9781987831375 (EPUB)

Classification: LCC PS8615.E437 L47 2023 | DDC C813/.6—dc23

Cover design by Nita Alvarez. Interior design and layout by Maywood Design.
Cover image by Inked Pixels, shutterstock.com.

Published by Wayshower Enterprises

https://www.tanishelliwell.com/
https://www.myspiritualtransformation.com/

Dedication

Everlasting gratitude to the elementals and their human partners who are restoring health and harmony to each other and to the Earth

Contents

Preamble

I'm sunken into a comfy chair in the sunroom of a wonderful old hotel overlooking the sea on the west coast of Ireland. I arrived in Keel on Achill Island a day ago for a short, much-needed holiday following two months working in Europe, and I was looking forward to country walks and meditation. In fact, I was getting ready for a full Irish breakfast when I heard a familiar voice.

"Tanis, I'd like you to write me life story now."

Perhaps I'd best give some background. Over thirty years ago, I lived in this same village of Keel in a cottage haunted by a leprechaun family. At that time, the male leprechaun, Himself, asked me to write a book about the experience, which I did, calling it *Summer with the Leprechauns*. The book is loved by many people and, since then, we have written four more books together and he is a regular visitor at my home for tea and porridge. Lloyd (that's the name Himself goes by with humans) now stands in front of me, looking as cocky as ever, talking to me about writing 'his' story on 'my' holiday.

Lloyd is about four feet tall, a little stocky with a sizeable paunch. He is dressed in traditional Irish leprechaun fashion, which includes a tight-fitting short, green jacket, brown woolen trousers cut off at the knee and coarse wool socks tucked into clog-like shoes, the size indicating that his feet are bigger than you'd likely see on a human. Completing his attire is his ever-present top hat. Can other people see him? Not unless they, like me, have got second sight. This is the gift—to be able to see beings, such as my leprechaun friend, in other realms.

"What about my holiday?" I replied, not keen, as you can imagine, to sacrifice that.

"Not a problem at all. You can write for three (pronounced *tree*) hours a day (he has a vague sense of time) and have a holiday for the rest."

"I have a lot of other books lined up calling my name," I answered, "so I don't need to add another to the list. How come you've never mentioned it before?"

"There'd be no point mentioning something whose time hadn't come, now would there?" Lloyd retorted. "You humans. Always living in the future rather than the present. Anyway, it will be easy," he added, opting for his most winning smile.

"How easy?" I'd heard this argument many times in the past, only to discover that his idea of easy and mine were worlds apart. "Anyway," I said, "I don't even have a computer here."

"Not a problem. I'll see to it." Lloyd replied, and immediately disappeared.

During breakfast, I mulled over my friend's idea. We've come a long way together and I've realized that whenever he requests that I write a book, I never know at the outset what the book will be about. Yet I've learned to trust the unfolding process and now appreciate, although with some trepidation, the expanded void of unknowing where something is born from the ethers. Which is why, as I popped the last morsel of soda bread into my mouth, I had already decided to accept his proposal.

With the precious time left for my shrinking holiday, I decided to enjoy the beautiful June day and to wander up Crumpaun Lane to see the leprechauns' cottage where I had lived so many years ago. Since then, the cottage had been sold to a Dublin family who was seldom there, which suited the leprechaun's family just fine. The owners were absent and, sure that they wouldn't mind, I let myself in the gate. I was wandering into the wild-flowered yard to greet my former home, when I heard you-know-whose voice echoing in the ethers: "I'm working on getting the computer."

Relieved that I was free to enjoy the day, I sank into the meadow, breathing in the fresh sea breeze that always blows in Keel, and I felt my heart fall into the deep, happy rhythm of rightness and sense of home that I always felt there. By late afternoon, having taken the long meandering path home down country lanes, I was once again nearing my guest house when I stopped to chat with a local woman walking her dog. Locals are curious about strangers and are keen to ask if they have any Irish connections, so I was asked my name. When I told her my first name, her ears perked up. "You wouldn't by chance have written a book about leprechauns?" she inquired.

"Yes, that's me," I answered, pleased that a local knew the book, and I surprised myself by adding, "and now the leprechaun wants me to write his story but I have no computer."

Beaming, the woman responded, "Well, I have the perfect solution for you. Tom, the next neighbor over, used to have a computer repair shop and he'd probably be able to fix you up with something."

This was surely the leprechaun's doing. After saying goodbye to her, I walked next door to Tom's place and found a middle-aged man of average height in an open workshop surrounded by computers in all states of repair.

"Hello, Tom," I said, introducing myself as I got closer, "I'm a writer staying next door and I need to write a book but I'm without a computer. Have you any I could rent?"

"What kind of book would that be?" he asked, curious.

"Promise you won't laugh," I replied. I'm always nervous introducing the topic of leprechauns when initially meeting someone, especially in Ireland, as I've found many Irish folks are sensitive about being associated with leprechauns for fear you're mocking them.

"I'll not laugh," he answered, smiling broadly.

"It's a book about my leprechaun friend who lives up Crumpaun Lane," I said, taking a chance.

"Oh, I believe that," said Tom. "Let me tell you a story… A few years back, a young woman brought in her computer to be fixed and I found a file deep down in the computer by someone called Mary, which was not the lady's name. When the young woman, a teacher she was, came to pick up her computer, I asked her, 'Who is Mary?' Well, she went weak at the knees, turned pale and told me she lived in a house that was haunted by an old woman who called herself Mary. So, you see, I believe you, and my wife could tell you lots of tales about these kinds of things around here. I'll see what I can do about your computer. Why don't you come back a little later?"

By now, it was clear that Lloyd had, once again, pulled off his bit of magic to find Tom, the absolutely perfect person, to be involved in his writing project. I walked back to the guest house to enjoy my last free evening, knowing that the leprechaun's story was a done deal. Sure enough, by the next morning, Tom had pieced together parts from two separate computers that he said were 'banjaxed'—an Irish term for totally broken. So here I am ready for Himself to tell his story.

Before I start, I'd like to say that there was a certain rightness about Lloyd choosing to recount his story at that time. I was back in Keel, the tiny village where I'd originally met him so long ago. In his cottage, his home, he had told me about elementals—nature spirits, if you like—and asked me to write about the importance of elementals and how he was part of a group that wanted to be partners with humans to heal the Earth. Writing that book changed my life and now it was time to find out more about *his* life. And I was happy to do so. So, on that beautiful late-spring morning, I took myself back to his cottage, got comfortable on the grass, and was all set when Lloyd sat down in front of me and said, "Ready for dictation? I'm glad you're keen to do this."

Then and there, without a word of introduction, the leprechaun launched in!

Leprechaun Childhood and the Old Way

Me story is important to record because the Old Ones are dying out and I'm part of a new generation that is starting to do things differently from our ancestors. To begin, then. I wasn't born in Crumpaun Cottage. I was actually born in a turf cottage. It had sods of turf on the sides and thatch for the roof. It wasn't really a cottage—more of a shed out the back of the human house, where me family and I were living. 'Twas a shed where the turf was stored and we also had the coos in there, and there were chickens comin' and goin' and layin' eggs in places they shouldn't be. And weren't the children of the house always comin' to look for them.

Now, it wasn't a rich family that had the house, nor was it poor. You'd say it was middle class and this was before all the troubles started in Ireland. I was born around the early 1840s. If you know your history, you'd know this was the time of the *An Drochshaol*, which means the hard times, as this was the time of the potato famine and the Great Hunger.

The reason I've not wanted to give me age before is that humans would have a hard time believing it. You see, leprechauns and most elementals are extremely long-lived. Also, time in your world and ours runs differently. This is why when humans used to come to our world and stay awhile, when they returned to their human world they'd find that a few hundred years had passed. Anyway, back to me story.

Ma and Da grew up in the old Ireland when humans believed in faeries and when the farmers put aside a section of their farm for the faeries to have their homes. I don't only mean leprechauns, which is the kind of elementals to which I belong. There have been elementals for all time, but that's what we prefer to call our race, just as you call yourselves humans. Anyway, there are all kinds of 'little people', which is another name you humans love to use for us, living all over the world.

Some elementals—field faeries or pixies, you might say—would live in faerie rings located in unplowed areas where humans never went. In these rings, there might be some old trees, such as the sacred hawthorn, blackthorn or gorse. The field faeries would stay on their ground and make merry and, when the full moon was up, some farmers coming home from the pub might hear them singing or see them dancing and sometimes they'd be meeting them.

There would be others of our folk living on the farm as well and some of them would be helping the farmers with the milking and getting the chicks to lay their eggs and generally lending a hand. Blessing the farm. Blessing the potatoes. And every morning in gratitude the farmer would leave out milk and bread and honey for them. We all got on great and Ma and Da grew up in that kind of environment. Very traditional, like. Da was a cobbler and prided himself on the shoes he could make. Other leprechauns would come and ask him his secret as they could not make them half as well. But Da would keep his secrets close 'cos leprechauns don't tell other leprechauns their secrets.

I was the eldest of four children and there were two boys and two girls in the family. Usually with elementals, the boys would be trained to keep up the Da's trade and the girls would be kept by the mother and trained in the kitchen to make food and mend clothes and darn socks. They'd also be the ones that would be gathering in the milk and washing the clothes.

I'd as soon move on in me story to the interesting part when I took to the road but I suppose you, being humans, want more detail about what it's like to be an elemental child. First of all, there's no such thing as one kind of elemental childhood. There are all kinds of elementals but, being a leprechaun, I can only speak with authority about us.

What all elementals have in common is the way they are as infants. From what I understand from studying humans, your infants are still connected to spiritual realms and see angels and great beings and even get a sense of what their purpose is in this life. Elemental infants, on the other hand, live in a world full of sensations, colored lights and sounds and feelings. Elementals have a strong emotional—you'd say astral—body, whereas humans have a strong mental body and ego, so this is why our experiences differ as infants. Gradually, elementals start to perceive the world around them more and grow consciously into knowing their physical body. This takes longer than it does for humans but, then again, our lives are much longer.

The next stage for humans and elementals is also different. Human children gradually lose touch with the spirit world and the beings in other dimensions that guide them. Elementals, on the other hand, become more conscious of the spirit realms and beings that guide them. Whereas you become locked in present time, elementals flow between past, present and future by only using thought, but in childhood, you'd say almost by instinct. Both humans and elementals incarnate more fully into their respective worlds as they grow up. For your folks, this means becoming more physical in the third-dimensional reality and, for elementals, it means becoming more physical in the astral world.

I'll explain what I mean. Childhood for both our races involves play. Before the age of about seven, human *leanbh* (I'll use yer word 'kiddies' or you might miss me meanin'), can see elementals and have us as play friends. Little human girls make tea parties with young elves and human parents go along with the 'fantasy'. The veil comes down for humans when they go off to school to learn about the 'real' world in which adults believe. By contrast, elemental children of the same developmental age actively play in many different astral worlds. Some with human ghosts and others with unicorns, dragons, satyrs and many other beings. When human kiddies are out playing and don't come home, their parents check with the neighbors; but when elemental kiddies don't come home, their parents search in the various astral realms.

When kiddies turn into young 'uns in the elemental world, they start hanging around elementals of their own clan and each clan specializes in a certain gift and no clan is more important than another. In the traditional elemental world, leprechauns, pixies, trolls, goblins, elves and others belong to a specific clan and perform a role in our society depending on their clan. For instance, a leprechaun would not think of taking up heavy metal work like the trolls. This is the way I was raised. It's changing now, and I'll get to that later, but I want you to understand how I was raised.

I started to be different from most leprechauns at a relatively early age. As a child, I often sat back and watched other children and adults rather than participating in what they were doing.

I liked to observe, not only leprechauns, but also goblins, trolls and different kinds of elementals. Why was I different? Well, in human evolution, you might say that an individual is formed in his or her present life by certain gifts and interests that are developed in past lives. In the elemental world, on the other hand, we'd say that there are energies that enter our world at certain times in history and that these energies, which you'd call universal consciousness, form a person. When I was born, there were new energies entering that were shaping me and other elementals to welcome a new way of interacting between us and humans.

When, using human measuring, I was about age nine up to teenage years, I was content to observe my local community in Keel. There was more than enough to learn here. When other young 'uns were playing, I'd often wander off to watch adults doing what adults do—leprechauns making shoes and being tailors and even doing some other crafts.

After a while, I thought I'd seen all that leprechauns did. You know how young 'uns are. Then I began to hang back to observe trolls when they were talking to each other or doing something. I even tried studying goblins but they were always on to me and thought I might be a spy for leprechauns, so they'd shoo me off. I gave it me best with field faeries but I couldn't keep up with their dancin' and singin' and they'd laugh at me. I was a bit sensitive to that. I didn't really fit in with other leprechaun children and they sensed that, of course, and so mostly ignored me, at least when I was young, when I tried to join them in games.

I even liked to observe female doings, and others would have thought that very strange. When Ma was teaching me sisters, I'd linger in the sitting room to overhear their conversation. Ma would be teaching them how to make bread and would be saying, "Ye need to add a pinch of salt or 'twill be useless and make sure to always give the man a fatter piece."

Moira, one of me sisters, would query Ma's instruction. "But what if he's done nothing and I've done the washing and cleaning, shouldn't I receive the larger share?"

"That's not to happen," says Ma, firmly. "The man's always got to feel special and it's our duty to make sure he does. That way, he'll be pleased to do favors when ye ask. He's honor-bound to agree."

I remember the day Moira got that lesson. When supper time arrived and I sat down for a piece of bread, didn't she turn to me and, extending the honey pot, say in her sweetest voice, "Dear brother, wouldn't ye like some honey for your bread?"

"That I would," I answered in me sweetest voice too, all the time thinkin', *What's this going to cost me?*

Sisters and brothers rarely talk to each other in their sweet voices, at least in me experience. However, glancing at Ma out of the corner of me eye, I could see she was mighty pleased with us both. As you can see, I learned a lot about females from listening to their conversations and how they thought. This stood me in good stead in later years with me own mate. Now, back to the story of teenage years.

I'd became an authority on females and other elemental clans and could tell good stories about them. Hence, as I got older, I carved meself a place with me peers. Around about that same time, I noticed that there were a few elementals in different clans, such as goblins and trolls, who seemed to be more like me and who didn't belong with their peers. We were suspicious of each other initially but, over time, we started to meet up a bit. This was not at all the elemental way, so we were considered strange in our community.

You must be wondering how our parents were taking this. Well, it depended. Some were trying to get a grip on us and drag us back into being 'normal' and others were letting us go our own way. It was the same with the Old Ones. Some were threatened by our unelemental-like behavior and saw us as a threat to their traditional way of life that had worked for thousands of years. Others, on the other hand, were feeling the new energies and were speaking up for us. Mind, I still saw meself as a leprechaun and wanted to be part of the community. So I didn't push too far and tried to be accommodating. But gradually it became clear that I'd need to find me own path.

Wandering the Road

Ordinarily, the Da in a leprechaun family would train the boys and teach his secrets. Me brother was happy to go that way but I never could get adjusted to it. You see, already I felt the wind changing in the human realm and conflicts coming between the Protestants and the Irish, or maybe it'd be more true to say the British and the Irish, or even more true to say the rich and the poor.

Our Old Ones had foretold that this would signal the end to our traditional way of life and that we elementals would have to go through a big change; a *diaspora* is what they called it. It would be a time of great chaos when the old way would end and the new way would not have begun and we'd be losing a lot of our people and our traditions. Over the last hundred years, we'd already seen that there were fewer farmers who respected the old ways and the areas where the elementals lived. In Ireland, forests were being cut down and elves were having trouble finding places to live, although in the west we'd been lucky that we'd not had to deal with this. Still, the bards were telling us that, across the sea in Britain, it was even worse, except to the west and the north of that isle. Therefore, we knew times were changing.

I wanted to be part of the new and felt that to stay with the old would help neither elementals nor humans. I knew inside meself that elementals had to work with humans in a new way and that keeping to ourselves was not the answer. In the west where I lived, humans and elementals had a kind of mutual understanding and even respect but we rarely had any real interaction. Oh, sure, we'd met humans who had second sight and would talk to us, but humans were starting to lose their second sight. This happened because they were more interested in new-fangled things, like machines, than in talking to elementals and in loving the Earth. Both humans and elementals started to keep to their own and there was not as much food being left out for us, and our homes and land were being taken away.

The long and the short is that I was looking for a change. The Old Ones couldn't help me as they were guardians of the old and Da was alright about me finding me own way. Not that happy about it, really, but he was alright. I was lucky to be born into the family I was and he had another son who would carry on his traditional trade. Elementals don't go to school the way humans do. We learn from our parents and take an apprenticeship from an early age—at least in those days we did. Our traditions are passed down this way.

We elementals inherit the memory of all the generations and, in the olden days, your human bards had a long memory like us and could read what humans call the Akashic Records or Book of Life. All elementals can read it, if they want to, but most elementals don't want to; they only want to keep the lineage of their own family alive and the trade that they do and pass along those secrets. This is the way we learn on the knees of our Ma and Da.

Me, now, I was born on Achill but, when I didn't pick up Da's trade, I started wandering. I went to the south of Ireland, around the lakes, to find out what other elementals had to say about their land and what was happening to them. Gathering their stories, I heard that elves were under siege as their forests were being cut, forcing them into smaller areas. This led to elven kings having more wars between themselves where they were killing off their own. Humans were also killing off their own to make space for each of their own traditions. Learning this, I was not happy.

I used to meet quite a few of the Old Ones when I traveled about and I especially liked to hear the elemental and human bards tellin' their stories. Many a night I'd take a seat in a pub so I could listen to human bards tell tales about wars and famous people, like the kings and queens. Truth be told, I was also trying to gain a little warmth off the peat fire and even a bit of Guinness. When some local fella was drinking his pint, I'd down a little swig at the end. Elementals can take the essence—the goodness—out of food, and I was taking the goodness of the Guinness. However, I've got me ethics. So, if I had a nip o' that fella's beer, I'd be sure to knock over his glass so he wouldn't be drinking what I'd just had the best of.

I became fond of sitting in pubs listening to yarns and got quite an education. I highly recommend it. By doing this, I started to get more interested in humans and realized that most of you are like us—people who are only striving to stay alive and do the best ye can for yer families. There'd be farmers talking about the failure of their crops, or too many children to feed and not enough food, and about the troubles. I mean the famines and problems with the potatoes.

Now, if you are doing your numbers, you'll know that I was born at the beginning of these hard times so you might be wondering how I'd be travelling around seeing all this as a young 'un. I'm going to make it clear. Elementals can travel in space and time and are not glued to a time and place like humans. Hence I could travel back and be part of that time that was affecting so many folks. Also, the potato blight happened again in the 1870s—not as bad that time, mind you, but enough that I wanted to see it in the earlier 1840s. So back I went. Anyway, getting on with me story.

You'd see field after field with the potato blight and whole families on the road with their cart and horse or just carrying their belongings on their backs. They were looking for work so they wouldn't starve and this was a very sad time. Some of the rich people did help and gave work and food, especially at the beginning when they didn't know how bad it was going to get. But as the blight passed to their fields, they became nervous about seeing strangers and sick folks, fearing they'd bring the problem with them.

This was a devastating time in Irish history and I wasn't getting much food either. I was getting quite thin but we elementals can go a long time without eating. We're not as dainty as humans. We can always get some nourishment from the sun, plants and even the air. So we weren't in the same terrible shape as some of your people.

Gradually, I met more elementals traveling. I discovered that I was not the only elemental on the road trying to figure out what the coming way would be. This was a little strange, as elementals, generally speaking, aren't like that. We tend to be born in one place and stay in that place. Meanwhile, I noticed that many of the elementals I met were quite knowledgeable and we started to have conversations. This wasn't normal either. Usually, leprechauns stick with leprechauns and elves stick with elves. But here I was having a conversation with an elf or a goblin or some field faerie and I started to make new friends.

When I was still new to being alone, I remember one evening, as dusk was turning to dark, coming upon a campfire just off the road.

Moving closer, but nonetheless keeping me wits about me and going silently, I saw a mixed group of elementals all sharing the warmth. The goblin saw me; they have the sharpest eyes and he motioned me over. "So, friend, come and join us."

"Don't mind if I do," I replied, edging closer, even though I was somewhat nervous with them gawking.

An older elf—older than me anyway, but that wasn't hard as I was only young—waved me over to a place at his side. "You're welcome to share a meal as we've been lucky today with donations from the local farmers."

"That's a stretch," volunteered the goblin who'd welcomed me. "They'll not know it was a donation till the morn."

"We're entitled to it," declared a brawny lad, a young troll, as he picked up his bowl and, head down, tucked in.

"I'm wondering if you're travelling together," I said, full of curiosity but not wanting to be pushy.

"Off and on," replied the elf, handing me some bread and nuts. It was easy to see that he was a wood and not a royal elf for he was dressed in dull greens and browns that blended nicely into the forest. "It depends where the breeze calls us and where our feet take us," he added, smiling as he took a bite of his bread.

I could tell from his accent that he was from the south and I reckoned not too far from where we were. Why then was he wandering around on his home turf, I was thinking, but was too polite to ask. Elementals, though, are mighty good at hearing others thoughts, so he picked up me unspoken question straightaway.

"I've kind of appointed myself a guardian for travelers," he offered. "You're right that I'm on the land I know best. Therefore, when I see strange elementals wandering the road, I feel honor-bound to lend a hand and teach them some wood skills."

"For instance, I hear in your speech that you're from the west and you look new to the road."

I was a bit offended that I looked like a beginner. We leprechauns are touchy about such things, especially with strangers. The others could see I was miffed and the goblin started laughing. "Don't take it personal, young'un," he grinned. "We all start somewhere and it's good you've met us worldly ones tonight to steer ye right." With those words, he burst out laughing and slapped his knee, chuffed that he could make a leprechaun humble.

"Don't take offence," inserted the elf, trying to keep peace. "Goblins love to find a weakness to insert their tongue. Conor here wasn't so expert a few moons ago that he need laugh."

With the elf's words, Conor became the color of the fire and turned his attention to his food. Taking the hint and with a fierce hunger on me, I dove into the bread as well. That's how I met me first elemental friends who later joined our group. From them and others, I started to learn more about the traditional way of life of various clans of elementals from different parts of the country and how life was changing for all of us. These elementals had the same idea as me and wanted to be part of the new way to preserve elemental homes and ways of life.

However, there was a split among the elementals I met. Not all of them wanted to work cooperatively with humans. In fact, maybe half thought humans were the problem, to be avoided at all costs. But the other half had lived on farms where the humans were half-decent and they'd got to trust them a bit. Or maybe these same elementals knew there was no other way.

It got to be that, when I met an elemental for the first time, I'd sort out pretty soon which way the gate was going to swing— towards liking humans or away from liking them. I started to limit my time with the elementals who wanted nothing to do with you folks. These elementals were using their energy for anger and negativity and trying to think of ways to trip up humans and cause you more problems. I reckoned you folks had quite enough problems without us causing more. In fact, you probably could use a helping hand. In this way, I was like Da and Ma. I'd had a good raising around humans so I had a bit more trust but, in some areas of Ireland, elementals hadn't been around humans for some time or they had problems with them recently. Still, if those angry elementals had tapped into their ancestral memory, they would have remembered the time when humans and elementals got along, but they weren't about to do that. This is what anger can do. It can blind you to the truth.

Time moved on and I'd been walking for a few decades, but I was still a young 'un. A few decades for elementals are like a couple of years for you. Also, your life spans then were much shorter than they are in the present day, so there was quite a difference between human and elemental lifetimes. Around about this time, when many of us elementals were wondering how we could work with humans, I started hearing about humans who wanted to work with elementals.

Now, I'd best fill in a little detail. Prior to the last few hundred years, there were many humans who entered the elemental world because, formerly, the veil between our worlds was quite thin and the portals between the two worlds were quite easy to pass through. Humans, like elementals, can manifest what they believe in and many of you believed in elementals and knew of portals where you could cross into the elemental world. A lot of bards crossed to get better stories and to learn ways of playing their harps and singing. We're the experts in these arts and humans have a long way to go. So bards were some of the most likely humans for us to meet in those days. Also, your bards used to travel all over Europe and gather these stories. They'd often be wandering on their own, so they'd be easier to approach, as they were interested in having a conversation with a knowledgeable elemental. Maybe I should also mention that there were always elves who were partial to you folks and who liked nothing better than to seduce you and bring you to our world. These are the ways that you folks came into our world prior to what you call the 19th century and this had been going on for a few thousand years.

But we were starting to get a new kind of human in the late 1800s that crossed into our elemental world. They wanted to strengthen elementals and to build bridges between our two worlds. These bridges were starting to break down with the breakdown of the traditions and, because of this, the portals were starting to close and these humans were trying to keep the portals open.

We elementals had been meeting what we referred to as 'healing' humans—both in our communities and whilst traveling on the roads. They said they'd like to work with elementals and over a few decades this became a strong theme. I started to see the same elementals and same humans turning up in the same places. When elementals have that kind of thing happening, we call it a node of power and we're attracted to these nodes of power. Because of this, we elementals wanted to talk to these healing humans to see what they were recommending.

By now, all of us elementals on the road had been gathering stories and had started to create our own theme. We'd been away from our traditions for a long while so, in a way, we were starting to form our own tradition. We were developing a different life purpose and were thinking that maybe humans and elementals could work together in a new way. One of the 'healing' humans was Rudolf Steiner, the founder of anthroposophy, who some of you know. When we originally met him, he wasn't that old. Only in his thirties, I guess you'd say. But he was very keen and a hard-working one. Anyway, I used to talk to him quite often.

Me Group

I'd like to talk about the group that was forming, which I came to think of as me group. We were mostly forest elves, leprechauns, field fairies and brownies, however some trolls had come down from the north and there were a couple of royal elves. We also had a few goblins in our group. I do mean 'a few' because, on the whole, goblins are not friendly to humans as you tampered with their evolution in earlier times. For this reason, goblins prefer to live in the wilds, far away from human habitations. If goblins do live near you, one of their pastimes is to make up games that they can play against you lot and goblins compete in developing clever games to trip you up.

When I say *trip up*, I mean, for example, that goblins have contests on a country lane to see how many humans they can manage to trip up in a week or in a month. So, if you aren't watching where you're going, a goblin might steer you into a pot hole and get your shoes wet. Or goblins would trip you on a lane to make you fall and cause little injuries. We're not saying mutilating or killing, we're only saying *trip up* and the game is actually called Trip up the Humans. This is one of the goblin pastimes.

You'd also find goblins hanging around inside a pub playing games to see who could drink the beer before the humans got to it.

They'd put wagers starting when the beer got put down in front of the human to see who could drink it before the human got his mouth to it. And the most daring goblins might even be crawling onto the counter to get the beer as it was being poured into the pint. But usually that would end up being a mucky mess.

You might be wondering what their wager was. In our kingdom, we use gold for money and each goblin would wager a gold piece and a 'neutral' goblin would be designated to judge which goblin won the contest. The judge, clutching a shillelagh, would climb onto the counter and knock it on the human's head and that would be another part of the game. All of a sudden, the human would end up with a mighty headache and wonder how he got it and 'tis likely it'd be the judge signaling who had won the wager.

Maybe you're thinkin' I've got it in for goblins. Leprechauns and goblins, 'cos we both think we're the cleverest ones, are known for competing in just about anything. Yet, truth be told, although I like to hold up leprechaun tradition, I've got a soft spot for several goblins, as you'll discover as I get further into me story.

Speaking of leprechauns, you wouldn't see any female leprechauns on the roads as it would be strictly against our traditions, but most of the elementals travelling would be males anyway. Occasionally, you'd see a female elf—a forest elf—as a female royal elf would have to have carriages and servants and the way the rest of us lived on the road was a bit too *rough and tumble* for the likes o' them. A female forest elf, on the other hand, would be able to take care of herself and find her own meals so there were some of them on the road.

Still, once, we did meet a female royal elf who was dressed like a forest elf. Us fellas could tell the difference right off, but she was having such a good time pretending she was a forest elf that we let her enjoy her game and let her join us for a while. This is how it happened. My leprechaun friend, Shamus, and I were making our way down the road through a forest when a female elf emerged from behind a tree and hailed us.

"Hello, fellas," she called out, waving.

Now, this was our earliest sign that she was a fraud. Elves sneak up on you and are so silent you never hear them emerge from a forest until they are at your side. She was dressed in brown and green and was taller than a usual forest elf too.

"Hang on," was her next cry as she made strides towards us.

The problem was that her obviously new shoes had never seen a stride before and were trying to accommodate her lunges. My friend nudged me in the ribs, a sure sign he was onto her game but intended to play along.

"Well, hello darlin'," Shamus called out. "Why don't you join us." There were two significant clues in our address that we had her number. First, you'd never address a forest elf, female or male, as 'darlin''. They can out-hunt and out-walk any leprechaun or troll, and are also better at finding their way in strange surroundings, so you treat them with respect. Second, if she was a royal elf, we should be saying, 'Your lady', whilst bowing and scraping. However, as she was pretending, we decided we'd pretend along with her as if she were a leprechaun lass and one of ours, very informal and casual-like.

"Gentlemen," she addressed us, bristling and trying to recover her dignity, "if you don't mind, I'm partial to accompanying you for a while."

"Not at all, darlin'," said Shamus, adding salt to the wound. "We're going to stop shortly and you can share our campfire, if ye like. But I'm curious as to where you're heading."

"Here and there," she replied, vaguely. "I thought I'd take time off from hunting and mushrooming and other forest work and see what's happening with other folk."

"We've a similar interest," I said, trying to include her more than me evil friend was doing. "We're interested in finding out what's happening in the human world right now and how elementals are affected. More to the point, what we can do about it."

"Exactly," she responded, breathing a sigh of relief at being accepted.

However, Shamus wasn't finished his teasing. "I'm right pleased you've joined us as we're hopeless at mushrooming and foraging in the forest for food and, expert as you are, you can do the foraging and we'll share our bread.

Her eyes went wild with terror at having to prove her claim to be a forest elf, so I took pity. "Sure, I'm not at all bad at mushrooming meself and I'll accompany our lass in the forest to prove it." With those words, signaling her to join me, I set out for the trees, shouting back over me shoulder. "You set up camp, Shamus, we'll bring the mushrooms."

Wasn't she relieved! She clung to me footsteps, stopping where I stopped, looking where I looked, and picking where I picked. In the end, she'd quite a bundle of mushrooms and I must say that, being a gentleman, I left the best ones for her to pick. Mind, I watched her closely, making sure she wasn't picking any special mushrooms that would be sending us on a trip to other realms. Even though the Druids ate the fruit, to 'go away with the faeries' and commune with the universe, there was a right time and place for this and, what with her being in a strange way already, it was best to keep her safe. As it was, she looked up after an hour and I could tell she hadn't a clue where we were or how to find her way back to our camp.

"I think we've enough. What do ye think?" I asked.

"Sure this is grand," she replied, distracted, and continued walking in circles and peering into the trees.

"Do ye want to lead us back?" said I, unable to resist having a little fun.

"Ummm, ahhh, it would be good for you to lead. With me being so tall, I might block your view," she answered, struggling to find an excuse.

"Right ye are, darlin'," I responded, knowing it was a stretch for a female royal elf to do what she was doing.

And so we journeyed with her for a few days and shared our campfire and even took her to a pub. The darlin' was trying, so we made it easy. She didn't fit in with other royal elves and I think she was interested in getting to know humans better. If I'm not mistaken, I think she might even have enticed a good-looking human male, who she was eying up in the pub one night, and taken him back to her realm for a while. For a spin, as we say, and neither she nor he was seen after that.

Elementals who were traveling, like our royal elf darlin', were all a bit unusual. Leprechauns are fairly sturdy and aren't used to covering much ground in a day, hence we wouldn't commonly be traveling with either male or female elves, of the royal or forest kind. In fact, many of us elementals were ranging by ourselves and would meet in nodes of power every few weeks or months.

You're wondering about these nodes of power, am I right? You'd call them leylines or dragon lines, and wherever these magnetic lines cross over on the Earth, there's a node of power. Anyway, all beings, whether they're consciously aware of it or not, are attracted or repulsed by nodes of power, and we've noticed that humans are keen on building temples and the like on them too. We elementals like to gather in them as our connection with universal forces is stronger there. We also like to do our rituals and conduct our sacred ceremonies there. So nothing could be more natural for the elementals on the road than to gather in these nodes of power to share yarns of what we'd been doing. That's the way we got to know the others, rather than by walking with them.

I enjoyed walking with Shamus, me leprechaun friend from the Midlands. He'd come west and I'd gone east and we'd met one day in one of these nodes. He'd been on the road as long as me and we got to talking. I don't mind telling you me friend's name as I don't think you'll be trying to get hold of him.

Shamus came from a farming community where they didn't have the special breed of coos that we have on Achill and, loving his coos, he liked to visit me island. Shamus had been raised on a farm around more humans than our family and he came on the road for the same reasons as me. He'd also left his home to figure out what he wanted to do… either to find a way to work with humans or to go home, choose a leprechaun lass, settle down and have a family. We used to talk about this as one of the great dilemmas facing us. Both of us were quaking in our boots about what it would be like if we totally disentangled ourselves from the traditional leprechaun way of life. We were wondering if we'd be ostracized and booted out of our respective leprechaun communities. We both worried about this and it was our main reason for hesitating about committing to partner with humans.

Shamus and I decided about the same time to return home and see how hard it was to fit back into the leprechaun community and, what's more, if we even wanted to. And, better still, if there was a possibility that we could have everything we wanted. Leprechauns are always hedging their bets and, if we could arrange it, we wanted both a wandering life and a home community. Therefore, Shamus and I agreed to return home but to stay in touch. As elementals can travel in space and time, this wouldn't be a problem. He could come to me or I'd go to him to find out what we'd decided to do. But I've got side-tracked. I was going to talk about meeting Rudolf Steiner. He, like us, was looking for a way to serve. He'd been one of the healing humans who crossed into our world, not only in this life, but also in other lives. We could read that on him because we can read all human lives on you. Just to mention... sometimes you folks think you're the only ones that reincarnate but we elementals reincarnate too. That's if we're at all interested in doing so and it's usually more the elves, leprechauns, goblins and trolls who want to become individuals with free will. Why? Because we need to develop our free will to become a full creator like humans are.

As you might know, elementals are experts at building form. We are etheric and astral beings and build form by working with the ethers from which all form is made. Elementals do this instinctively and follow the patterns that already exist in the ethers. We strongly identify with being members of a group, so we follow the patterns that our clan has already laid out. But as we become older, 'cos we live hundreds of years, we may become bored creating the same patterns and develop a desire to create something new. This is the beginning of individuating and some elementals start wishing to live beyond their current life so they can create new forms in another life. All these desires are stored in the ethers and the great beings, who oversee elemental evolution, give us what we wish for. Thus, we receive another life.

Then, when we reincarnate, we begin to develop a stronger mental body and an ego, just like a human has an ego. We start to work consciously to build our own unique personality, complete with a physical, emotional and mental body. This takes donkey's years as many lives are needed to accomplish this goal. And this is why only well-developed elementals, like elves and leprechauns and goblins, take on the job. Let's not forget that elementals are naturally beings of fun and joy. What I'm describing is hard work. No two ways about it. That's why it's not for all of us.

Me Da has reincarnated several times but me brother not as much. Me Da wanted to have a young 'un who'd follow his tradition and become a cobbler. He knew, even before I came in, that it wouldn't be me and I'd be willful and want to go me own way. You see, elementals can read the kind of children they're going to have. When elementals are deciding they want to have a child, they read the ethers to see the choices and the more developed they are, the more they can choose which child they want. Yet some of us unborn elementals up there could be a wee bit more insistent than others wanting to be born and so we may sort of twist the Da and Ma's arms to get the family we want. Of course, this is done with the guidance of the great beings who oversee our evolution.

Me brother was not near as willful as me and, accordingly, Ma and Da accepted one of each. They got one who would follow the old tradition, me brother, and one that would follow the new, which was me. You could say they were hedging their bets. This way, me family couldn't help but end up on the winning team, whatever happened. Making sure that they are going to end up on the winning team is another thing that leprechauns are particularly good at.

Sometimes, we come to a crossroads in evolution and you're never quite sure which path will succeed because, at some point, the energies look about equal. Evolution goes through rises and falls but it's usually the path bringing the new order that will triumph in the long term. You can for sure see that in human evolution but it's true in our own elemental kingdom too. Right now, we're coming out of a bit of a dip and we're starting to make progress into the new. This is what I'm most interested in.

I'd like to tell you about why I chose me Ma and Da. Of course, if you're a leprechaun, you're going to be born into a leprechaun family. Still, I wouldn't want it any other way, nor would most elementals, as we mostly like to stick with our own clan. Now, Ma and Da were quite developed, as leprechauns go, and this is how they chose each other in the first place. We're attracted to those who have compatible frequencies with us and are magnetized to those folks. So, it was as natural as breathing that they'd form a good bond.

In the same way, I was attracted to them 'cos from the higher ethers I could see they both had brighter lights than a lot of other choices I had for parents. They were not only developed, but also developed in the right way for me. They were flexible and open and tolerant and non-judgmental—all qualities I knew I needed in a family so as to do what I wanted in the coming life. Mind, at the beginning, I didn't know what that was but I knew I had to have the right ingredients to make the form, the life, I'd need. That's what I mean by how elementals work with the ethers to build the form they want. Humans do it too, only most don't know they're doing it.

We magnetize folks and opportunities to us—you call them synchronicities—and this was happening to me. Wandering on the road, I started to meet visitors from other countries who came to Ireland to see what was going on. That was quite interesting. But another thing. Not all these 'visitors' were of either elemental or human evolutions but were of other evolutions.

But I'd best back up or I'll lose you. I sometimes forget humans can't see what I'm talking about with me story. For elementals, words create images just like a holograph. Anyway, back to what I mean by 'other evolutions' visiting our elemental realm. I spoke earlier about Steiner, a human, coming to help elementals and he isn't the only human we've met in our realm. There are also beings from many other evolutions who visit our elemental world and they come as helpers, ambassadors or observers. Me friend Tanis and I have written a book called *Hybrids: So you think you are human,* where we talk about twenty-two different kinds of beings, including elementals, who have either incarnated into human evolution and/ or have visited our elemental realm.

Some of these are star beings, such as our great God Pan, who is the god of elementals. He's been with us forever in higher realms helping our evolution and he has come closer to Earth in these last thousand years or so. He's our equivalent of your Christ. Pan is helping implement the changes in our elemental evolution that allow us to enter human evolution, if we choose to do so, and if we've a strong enough individual identity not to lose ourselves in the human world. Pan also helps the group, to which I belong, to develop the strength to work with humans as co-creators and equal partners. So I'm particularly indebted to him.

Elemental evolution is changing now to work together with human evolution more than it did previously. This is starting to become a major theme for elementals and, I'd have to say, a lot of this change is due to the group that I became a part of in the latter 1800s. This is when elementals really started to work with this idea. In my years, I've lived through a lot. Although I look middle-aged to you, I'm teetering on the edge of the grave if you calculate me life in human years. Luckily, in leprechaun years, I'm still hale and hearty and that's the way I hope to keep it for a good time yet.

Courting

I was getting tired of walking the roads of Ireland since, by then, I'd been doing this for more than 20 years and was ready for a rest. Me Ma and Da lived in Keel on Achill so I thought I'd come back home to collect me thoughts before making any rash plans. This is a very leprechaun thing to do being as we're a cautious people. I'd come to a fork in the road. I'd either have to come back to Achill and live the life of a traditional leprechaun and find me place in the community or I'd have a more wandering life working with humans and other elementals in trying to find a way to go forward together. So I thought, before acting, I'd best go back and reflect.

That's how it happened that, one day, I was walking down Crumpaun Lane and saw a homey-looking cottage with smoke from a lovely peat fire coming out the chimney. There were a few other cottages on the lane at that time but this was one of the oldest and the others are gone now. Hence I moved to Crumpaun Cottage where I still live and this is near a hundred years ago. The only reason the cottage is still there is that we've set it up that way. We've arranged to be with humans who wanted to look after the cottage and who would give us some peace and quiet, so we could carry on together.

I'm saying 'we' at this moment but, when I came back home, I was alone. There wasn't a 'we', as I'd not found a mate, me female self, and our two little 'uns weren't born. Nonetheless, I was getting to the age when a leprechaun would be doing this.

We have matchmakers in our community and, when I returned to Achill, there was a matchmaker who talked to Ma and Da about setting me up with a mate. This was a bother, a distraction, as I was trying to collect me own thoughts and was not really looking for a lass. I couldn't be sure that anyone would suit me as I'd changed so much. Ma and Da were hoping to fix me up with someone traditional that would keep me home, but they were only dreamin'. It wasn't like I was ever going to be traditional, but you know parents, always in denial about their little 'uns.

However, as it happened, there was one leprechaun lass wandering around the village that caught me eye. Normally, lasses stay at home with the other women and don't go out much. But this one was taking walks by herself and she looked to be about me age, hence I was a wee bit curious. Now, you don't want to let on that you're interested, 'cos as soon as you do, the matchmaker will be at the door and you're hooked.

Accordingly, being a bit crafty, I'd arrange to be out walking at the same time as she'd be out walking. That way, I'd get a closer look as I'd be passing by or, as we like to say in leprechaun land, I'd get a better feel of it. Those words speak the truth for us because, when elementals meet each other, they get the feel of exactly what the other person is like, what their interests are and what they don't like. In a split second, we pick up all that information and more. It's really a *known*. You could say it's clairvoyance, clairaudience or clairsentience. I know that's the way you humans like to talk, but we'd say it's a *known*.

I could sense as I passed her by that she was getting the feel of me as well. It was kind of a joint thing as no words had been said and we hadn't stopped to talk as that would be serious. We both knew that we had an interest in each other and we had to figure out the next step as we could feel that neither one of us wanted to go to a matchmaker. Now, this way of acting was untraditional right there. To think of not going to a matchmaker to fix you up with the best possible mate was unthinkable in the leprechaun community, but here we both were thinking the unthinkable. It interested me even more when I discovered that she was so daring that she would think the unthinkable. That raised me estimation of her another notch.

She and I sent a telepathic message to each other to meet up. This was really breaking with tradition and, if we were caught doing it, we could get into buckets of trouble. It was harder for her because people were used to me wandering around, but she, being a lass, would have to make an excuse about why she was leaving the house. Turns out, it wasn't hard, as she already had a reputation for taking country walks and wandering off into the deserted village. Accordingly, she told her folks that she needed a bit of air, whilst she told me telepathically that she'd meet me on the cliffs of Minaun as, it being remote, there wouldn't likely be anyone up there at that time.

When we met, we made sure that we held off a goodly distance from each other so, if anyone caught sight of us, they'd not see us touching in any way. As was proper, I started the conversation with, "I'm pleased to meet you and thanks for coming."

To which she responded with, "I'm pleased to meet you and thanks for coming."

So far, the conversation wasn't very exciting but I could tell that she was trying to be proper and to hold a bit back in reserve and I respected her even more for doing that. She was already taking a big risk and was showing me that she wasn't a likely lass to have a tumble and that she was taking our meeting seriously. I didn't need to ask her where she lived, as I'd previously spotted her coming out of a cottage in the village, therefore I searched for the next thing to say.

"It's a nice bit of weather we're having," I said. Always a safe topic and a good way to begin.

She responded with, "Aye, nice that we have a bit of sun today."

Now, her comment was already a deviation, as 'twas not conventional. She was really telling me that she could express her own point of view at the same time as she was showing that she agreed with the first part of what I'd said. There was more to this simple conversation than you'd be thinking and you've got to have a leprechaun translate for you what was really meant.

Thus I thought I'd go a bit into what I was really interested in, so I countered with, "Ye may not know, but I've been off wandering for some time."

To which she responded, "I've heard that."

What she was saying was totally non-committal. She wasn't stating that she felt good or bad about me way of life. What she was really imparting was, "You're going to have to go on man and commit yourself to taking a stand."

So I went on and responded, "I found out quite a bit wandering away from the community." What I was really saying was, "You're going to have to step forward to ask me what it is and I'm going to see if you've enough gumption to do it."

Then she said, "I'd be interested in hearing what ye found out."

Well, that was unbelievable that I'd found a lass who'd think like a man and who'd express herself like that. I confess I was stymied for a minute and started to get nervous 'cos, if I was to take a mate, I'd want her to stay home and not be on the road with me. She'd be making me meals, looking after the home, and raising the little 'uns, so I could go off journeying. Accordingly, I had a real dilemma. Part of me was thinking, *You'd best turn and run in the opposite direction, man. She's maybe too much for you.* But then I felt into meself and discovered that I'd taken a risk in everything else I'd done for the last twenty years, so I might as well take a risk in choosing a mate.

I knew she was hearing all I was pondering and I could hear her thoughts too, of course. She was nervous and blushing and was thinking she'd gone a little too far in trying to interest me in herself. She was shaky 'cos she was interested in me. Well, as soon as I saw that, me heart opened and I thought, "This one is a treasure. She will be one I can cling to. One that will love me as I am and not try to change me. She's taking these risks 'cos she loves me."

So me heart was full open and I said to her, "Lass, I can see we're well matched. You've got courage enough to live the life you'd be living with me and I've got courage enough to ask ye."

I get teary just thinking about it. Humans think leprechauns don't have strong feelings and affection for another. However, I can tell you we feel things deeply. That's why we don't often talk about our personal lives being as it's too personal for us, too close to the heart. Consequently, we like to keep our feelings secret. Nonetheless, I know it's important to share me secrets with you humans who are following me story, that's why I'm taking a risk in telling you.

The lass and I didn't touch and kept ourselves totally pure so that anyone who met us wouldn't be able to tell anything in our energy. Our first decision together was to bypass the matchmaker and go straight to our parents. We decided to start with me Da and Ma as they were already used to me being odd. This different way of choosing a mate would only be one more odd thing that I'd done. They'd been able to accept all the other odd things, so it was a good bet they'd accept our untraditional way of courting.

Hence, we walked together to me parents' cottage. The lass was shaking like a leaf as her reputation held on a thread based on how me parents would receive her and accept or reject her. If our Das and Mas didn't accept us, we'd be kicked out of the leprechaun community. Although that would have been alright for me, she would have had to come on the road with me and this is not what she wanted. She wanted me and a family and also the exciting life I could give her.

When Ma saw us walking up to the gate, she ran into the back room and started praying to all the ancestors and everyone and everything she could think of. She was even saying, "Even if there are humans whose prayers are working, I'm praying to whoever you are praying to, as me son is bringing back a female and I know his Da is not going to like this."

Ma realized better than Da that I was going to need a mate who was different. She knew that the lass walking in the gate with me was different for there'd already been talk about her. Even though she was a good-looking lass, leprechaun lads that would want her, as she was so independent, would have been rare. Ma was thinking all these thoughts as we were coming in the gate and she was hoping that me Da would be alright. Ma didn't dare go to me Da and talk to him before I got there; that just wasn't done, but she was sending some telepathic messages, I'd say.

Da didn't see us as he was around the back cobbling his shoes, but he was picking up distress from Ma 'cos she was so flummoxed that she was sending many different messages and prayers. Thus Da was getting himself concerned before he knew what was going on. Asking the lass to wait out front, I went around the back so I could have a talk with him before he met her.

I started the conversation like this. "Fawder." Now he knew for sure he was in for it 'cos I was so formal and I'd me hat in me hand. "I've come asking for something important to me. I've met me mate, the one I'm wanting."

Now he started to boil as he was picking up what I was going to say before I got out the words. He leapt off his stool and began to walk towards the front of the cottage. That's when I did something leprechaun children seldom do with their parents. I touched his arm to stop him. "Fawder, listen to me! This is the lass I want and, if ye refuse her, we'll have to leave this community. Ye know it and then ye won't be seeing me again. But if ye want us in this community, ye'd best accept her 'cos I'll not have another."

Well, it took a lot out of me to speak to him like that and a lot out of him to hear it but he was an honorable man who knew I was serious and he didn't want to lose me. He was actually proud of me. Even though he wouldn't be talking to me about it, I'd hear him defending me to some of his mates who would be criticizing me for not staying around and being a proper cobbler. When he heard that, he'd defend me and what I was doing and say, "I'm hedging me bets," so that they'd think of him as crafty. At the same time, I was causing dissension in the community for I was starting to affect the young 'uns. Some were coming to listen to me stories about the life on the road and how we leprechauns and elementals had to adjust to the changing times.

All these thoughts were happening in his mind in one go until he had a realization. He recognized that, if he let me have this lass, not only would I stay in the community but also I'd be demonstrating that I wanted to settle down. This action would calm some of the young 'uns as well as the Old Ones who'd be thinking, "He's not so young and reckless. He's actually wanting to settle down and have a family and live here." Me taking a mate would have a peaceful effect on the community and he wouldn't lose me. All these thoughts were going on in his mind in a flash. Leprechauns are famous for being able to juggle thoughts ahead of other elementals and, I dare say, better than most humans.

Within a second, he came out with, "Right. I'd best meet her and see what I think."

He sauntered around to the front, nonchalant as you like, and did something very odd, really counter to tradition. He called out his mate from the cottage. Me Ma most likely had been listening at the door to hear our conversation, but she'd never let on. The moment she opened the door, he said to her, "Listen, we've got some company and I think we'd best be offering some tea."

Smiling at me lass, Ma showed her in and gestured for her to sit on a stool as the honored guest. And praising all the saints, the ancestors, the Great God Pan, and thinking her prayers had been answered, Ma ran to put the kettle on for tea. I was proud of me Ma and Da at how far they'd stretched in those 20-plus years I'd been on the road, to go from being traditional to this. But I guess they'd stretched way back before I was born. Knowing I was going to be willful, they welcomed me into their lives and here they were stretching more. That's the way me lass was welcomed into me family's home.

With a quick natter, it was arranged that me Ma and Da would go together to speak with her parents. They told her, "Go home and say to your parents that there'll be company coming shortly with an offer for you."

She did as they requested with a light heart, knowing that half the battle was won. I stayed in the cottage as only me Ma and Da would go. As the lass's parents were more traditional, it would have been too much to see me at that moment. It was already strange that Ma was going with Da and doubly strange that there was no matchmaker doing the honors.

Ma and Da put on their best clothes and yer man had on his good hat so that her parents would see they were getting a formal call. When my parents arrived, the tea was ready and bread was being baked. The dear young lass, who I was going to make me mate, had been able to block all thoughts of me from her Ma and Da. She had a strong will. I was proud of her. She was working to give me Ma and Da the chance to make it right. Her parents knew something was up but, in the beginning, they took it as a bit of a prank that the lass was playing.

When me Ma and Da arrived, they were invited to sit on two stools by the peat fire. Da started by saying, "Your daughter is a good-looking lass and she has a unique personality. I've been admiring her around the village and we're wanting a good mate for our son who is also a bit willful. Still, he wants to stay in the community and I was thinking that your lass and our son would make a good pair. And I was wondering if this suited youse."

Her parents were a bit surprised, but it couldn't have been too much of a shock as, over the years, they'd seen how that lass was. Truth be told, her Ma and Da were mighty relieved but they couldn't let on and had to pretend that they'd the dearest gem in the world and that I'd be stealing her away from them. This, being clever, was so they could negotiate paying only a small dowry.

Both fathers entered into the negotiation and me Da said, "Me son's already got a cottage."

Her Da countered, "But he's got no cattle, no sheep, nothing to give milk and, him being such a wanderer, he doesn't have a human who's likely to be giving him food. And then what will be happening to our lass?"

But me Da did his best and answered, "He might be going away, that may be true, but ye can see, he always comes back and he can always provide for the lass." To be fair, I wasn't much of a deal for a traditional lass. Therefore, Da wasn't pushing hard in the negotiations as he knew I was a hard sell as a prospective mate.

At this moment, me lass's Ma started to fidget 'cos she was worried that her mate was making too much of a fuss and might wreck this chance for their lass. Her Da could read her Ma's thoughts and knew that there'd probably be no more offers coming, the lass being so different, so he reluctantly gave in and said, "Then, let's strike a deal."

The men slapped hands on it. And you might be wondering what the woman were doing when the men were negotiating. They knew well enough not to interfere with men's business… at least, directly. But they were busy giving each other the nod, talking without talking, and making it clear by women signs that they were all for the match. Of course, the two men couldn't help but pick up on this.

Next, the two families had to decide what to do about the matchmaker. She wouldn't be happy to be cut out of the deal and would still want the gold from making the match. Neither of the parents wanted responsibility for giving the gold and decided to put it back in me yard to come up with the gold for the matchmaker. Unfortunately, that was a dilemma for I didn't have much to offer except the cottage.

Getting the Gold

B y now, I'd no doubt that the matchmaker had picked up the news that we'd be broadcasting in the ethers. Therefore, as quickly as I could, I dressed in me best and polished me shoes till they shone and set off to her cottage to make amends. She lived in the center of the village in the middle of the comings and goings where she could hear the local gossip and get her foot into any matchmaking opportunity at the earliest hint. You have to be enterprising if you're a matchmaker and it's a trade like any other. Her cottage had a lovely little fence around it with lots of multi-colored flowers in her garden. She'd a creative flare, probably more like a royal elf would have, if you ask me, but who am I to judge. So I unlatched the gate, sauntered to her door, and knocked.

"Coming," she called in her sweetest voice. Taking off me hat, I held it as she opened the door. Seeing me, her smile soured. "Arrah, so 'tis ye," she said, sucking air through clenched teeth. "I suppose you'd best come in as I don't do business at the door."

She pointed me to a stool, never offered me tea, and kept standing herself, a clear sign of her discontent. "I've heard that you've made a match without me. What do ye say for yourself?" she attacked with her tongue.

"You're very good at your trade—there's no one better, in fact," I began, hoping me charm would work. "And I know ordinarily you'd find any lad the best match but I'm a bit different than your usual lads and the lass, ye must agree, is different too. Consequently, you'd have had no end of trouble finding either of us the right match."

"So with your kind heart, you decided to save me some work, is that what you're claiming?" she said, placing her hands on her hips and scowling. "I'm not buying what you're selling, lad, and you'll have to pay more now that you've botched me reputation."

This was not going well. As leprechauns are firm respecters of each other's trade and would never trespass on another's territory, all the leprechauns would be agreeing with her. Once again, I'd crossed boundaries which, to their way of thinking, I shouldn't be crossing.

"Of course, I want to pay for your trouble," I said, looking up at her with me best smile before continuing, "but I'm a bit short of gold right now."

"I've heard enough outta you," she cut me off. "I want double me usual fee and I'm not waiting for years for it either, so you'll need to get it. Otherwise, it's your reputation will be sullied round these parts."

There was no mistaking that I had no bargaining power and that I'd have to get the gold somehow. Cowed, I took what was left of me pride, rose from the stool and made for the door, saying as I walked, "You'll get it. I'll see to it. Me word is good."

The question then was how to get the gold. I sent me future mate a telepathic message asking her to meet me in the same place on the cliffs as before, 'cos I required her help in devising a plan. I needn't tell you that I was now dragging her further down the NEW path by doing this. It's for the lads not the lasses to make decisions in the leprechaun world. Nonetheless, she joined me almost immediately.

"I've been to the matchmaker," I said, blushing with shame, "and she's doubled the usual matchmaking price for all the trouble I've caused."

"Ye mean 'we've caused'. I chose as well," she replied, saving me pride and letting me know she was committed through bad as well as good times. Wasn't I the lucky one!

"I thought we could go over the options on how to get that much gold. Ye might think of something that I've not thought of."

"Go on, then," she replied, waiting for the man to start.

There are several ways to do this if you're a male leprechaun and she might not know of them all, so I thought to appraise her of the options.

"One option would be to find out where another leprechaun hoards his gold and dig it up and steal it," I began.

"That would be crafty—clever even—but more the way a goblin would go about it, wouldn't ye say," she asked, in her sweetest voice.

"I've come to the same conclusion," I asserted, knowing it would be sneaky and there wouldn't be much pride in doing it that way.

"The second way would be to take gold off a human," I stated. "What if I go to a pub and wait till a human lad puts some gold on the counter to pay for a drink. I could launch in and take it before the bartender does. Making it disappear, like."

"Aye, but that would cause a fight between the human and the bartender, 'cos one would be saying he'd paid and the other would be saying he hadn't. That way would be dishonorable, wouldn't it?" she inquired, knowing full well I wouldn't choose a path with no honor.

"The third way to get the gold would be to earn it but, darlin', I'd have to settle down and become a cobbler or work with leather bags and clothing. It could take years for me to get enough gold, and would ye want that for me?" This was a test question to see if she wanted me happiness more than to be handfasted and I waited in suspense to hear how she'd answer.

"Aye, it's an option," she began, having some fun making me wait for her decision. Then, pausing, with a smile lighting up her pretty face, she continued, "Yet you'd not be happy and so it's not an option."

These abandoned choices left me short of ideas on how to get the gold and she could see I was stymied.

"Let's find a fourth option," she exclaimed, excited. "We've done everything in our courtship in a new way, so let's think of a way to get the gold that's not been done before."

Wasn't she a brilliant one. Thus, we put our heads together and, as they say, one plus one equals three. That's how we discovered a grand plan.

In them days, gold and silver was transported by coach and the coaches stopped at rich houses. Accordingly, I decided to get some of that gold. This would be taking money off the rich and not the poor and, although it wouldn't be that easy, me trump card was that humans couldn't see me.

Therefore, I was ready for the coach when it stopped at the pub to pick up passengers and I'd made sure to pack some sandwiches and tea to enjoy the journey. Elementals only need to think of where they want to go and they'll be there, but I was set on getting the most fun from me expedition by traveling like you folks do. We traveled for some time until the coach finally drove through the gates to a big house—me destination—and that's where I got off. As it was still light, I hung around outside and hid from the house brownies, who would definitely be able to see me and who'd be protecting the owners. I also hid from the goblins in the area who, feeling that anything in the house was theirs for the taking, would resent me as an intruder in their territory.

I ate me sandwiches and had a snooze and, when the night was well on and everyone in the house, even the elementals, were asleep, I snuck into the house. We leprechauns have got good sight in the dark and I was looking around to find the gold. Thinking the master would be keeping his gold close to his chest, I found me way into the biggest bedroom. There, yer man was snoring away and, bad luck, his big dog spotted me and started to growl. I practiced me best invisible trick of popping to a higher frequency and, luckily, the master quieted the dog and both went back to sleep. Using me intuition, I found his pouch under the bed—when will you folks ever learn? It had plenty of gold in it, which I stuffed into me jerkin, and softly exited the house.

Under cover of darkness, I crept down to the gate and waited till morning when a cart came out the gate on its way to market. Didn't I just hop unto that cart and go to market to get a few goodies for the larder on me way back home. I would call that a good night's work. I didn't feel bad about taking the master's gold as he already had too much and would be only saving it for the fun of himself and his rich guests. It was doing yer man a favor by relieving him of the burden of bad karma by using the gold for something that would do some good.

I showed me Da the gold as a bit of a brag and he was that proud of me ingenuity. Naturally, I shared the credit about me lass's part, so he'd be doubly proud that I'd got a smart one. Not wasting any time to pay me debt, I told him I was off to the matchmaker and, this time, he insisted on accompanying me. Why? He felt it was important to have a witness in case she denied that I'd ever given her the money. The community would have had a hard time believing that I'd been able to come up with the gold so quickly and might have doubted me. Me Da thought I'd done well and had set a new course—now called *option four*—for other leprechauns to get gold.

Not that the matchmaker was pleased to see me! She was cross for she had in her mind that she'd get even more gold than she'd asked for. She'd receive the first amount when I paid me debt and then the same amount another time when she denied she'd got anything. Nevertheless, in leprechaun land, I'd been crafty and hence the matchmaker had to respect me cleverness.

Our matchmaker, as you might have guessed, was a leprechaun lass who'd never found a mate. She was that sour; she never got picked; no juicy apple her. Matchmakers come from unmarried crones in the village. You might be tempted to ask, "What do they know about making matches when they never had one of their own?" We'd a tried and true solution to make certain that not one leprechaun was ever left without a trade and there was an apprenticeship for everyone. Thereby, when a lass got to a certain age and had not been asked by a lad, she'd go for an apprenticeship and learn the matching craft. That would be her trade.

It was a good trade and a matchmaker could live in comfort and be independent, which was unusual for a female. Still, this matchmaker didn't like the fact that I'd chosen to seal the match a new way and she could see her livelihood going out the window. Thus, she was opposed to me in principle. If I were in her clogs, I'd have to say that this was a fair assessment. Nevertheless, I'd paid, so I could get handfasted.

A Man-to-Man Natter

We had to wait awhile until we could carry out the handfasting—our elemental equivalent of marriage. Leprechauns don't like to be rushed. The problem was that we couldn't carry on our courting in secret like we'd been doing. I was thinking that even though I call her me lass, I've never told you her name. We leprechauns never give our real names, names being power, but me lass gave me a name for humans to use: Aine, pronounced *awn-ye*. 'Tis not far off her real name and she's right comfortable with it as it means 'brightness and splendor' in Irish and we had a queen of that name. I must say, Aine suits her.

Aine's Ma insisted that whenever we went walking either she or an auntie would walk with us. No touching. That was a fast rule. So we couldn't talk, natural like, and get to know each other better. We knew we had to abide by the restrictions as the whole community was watching us now to see what we were going to get up to next. We'd become that public. This doesn't suit a leprechaun at all 'cos we're very private. I suppose you'd say secretive but, no matter what words you use, neither of us liked the staring and whispering when we were out.

It was harder for her as she was the lass. Us lads don't have the same restrictions. Also, 'tis true to say that me Da knew I'd been carrying on for decades as a free man and wasn't going to be roped in by him or anyone, so he wasn't bothered. Well, maybe there was one conversation. Quite embarrassing, really. Here's what happened.

Da was quite the maker of *poitín*. Do you know what that is? It's made with potatoes and honey and a bit of spit to get it started. Of course, there's the secret ingredients that I won't be telling. Then you wait for it to brew. Our family's been making it for a few hundred years and we've a good reputation. It's only the men that would be drinking it as it's too strong for the lasses. And sometimes we give a nip to the sheep, if they're ailing, to set 'em right. It's got quite a kick and can heat you right up on a cold day.

Humans would be using a still to cook the poitín but that's not in the least necessary and we've done it for eons in a pot. A bit about the brew. You've got to watch it closely, for two reasons. First, your neighbor would be knowing where it was kept and could pop in and take it when you weren't looking. Humans might be thinking this was stealing but we don't see it the same. We see it more like a game. Who's the crafty one who can do it quick in the night and get home free? That would mean the loser would have to think of a crafty way to get back at the perpetrator. This game can go on for decades and even be passed on to children. We've even contests, and leprechauns, who are enormously crafty in the most complicated games, are famous and their names have been handed down for generations.

The second reason to watch the stewing pot is that it's been known to blow and you wouldn't know what could happen then. Maybe 'twould take down the shed. I know it's been said poitín could strike you blind but I never saw that happening. However, I have seen yer man many a time in the morning after consuming the night before and it's not a pretty sight.

I know I was saying that the lasses wouldn't have poitín, but sometimes I think they sneak a nip or two or five. We men wouldn't let on in the morning when they were not on top of their game. Well, maybe a nudge would be alright or, when they burnt the porridge, we'd say, "Porridge is a bit different today." That would normally straighten 'em out and, if that didn't work and they messed up with the dinner, we'd comment, "Think I'll go out back and check the poitín." That was bound to work.

I can hear you asking, "Do any leprechauns have problems holding their drink?" Of course, 'tis the same as everywhere—no better, no worse.

Anyway, as I was saying, I was visiting me Ma and Da's place when he says to me, "Let's go out the back awhile."

I knew by his tone that I was going to get some advice and wondered what that'd be. "*Ceart go leor,*" I said, which is Irish for *okay, fine.* You've got to know we're not talking English but Gaeilge (which some call Irish Gaelic), even though you hear us in English.

Out the door we went. He sauntered over to stand on one side of the poitín, whilst I stood on t'other. "Shall we see how she's coming along?" he asked, reaching into the pot with a ladle.

"Aye," says I, keeping open to his next move as he handed me a full glass.

"'Tis fair ready," I said, taking a nip. "What d'ye think?"

This gave yer man plenty of reason for drinking and I could see by the size of the glass he'd passed to me that he was planning a long recitation. Maybe it's a good moment to talk about our recitations. The Irish are famous for them. Elementals never had books. We had no need 'cos we've excellent memories and can remember entire stories, word for word, that are told by our bards. Because we can travel in space and time, we can go and hear the original bard say the story, and our bards make it a lifetime study doing just that, although often stories get added to by others. We can recite the story, never missing a word and hardly taking a breath. Therefore, when I mention that Da was planning a recitation, I mean that he'd obviously rehearsed something to say and me ears were growing waiting for him to begin.

"Son," he said, "I'm going to tell you what me Da told me and his Da before him." With these words, he started rocking back and forth, shifting his feet from side to side getting a rhythm going and moving into story-telling mode.

"It's a secret that we men keep and never let it leave the clan."

By now, I'm holding me breath wondering what's going to be said. What secret could I possibly not know? I'm not bragging when I say leprechauns are really proficient at ferreting out secrets, and I'm as good as the next one and maybe a bit better, and I'd no idea what was coming.

"What I'm going to recount must never ever be told to *any* female, on pain of death," he continued, giving me a no-non-sense glower.

Curious though I was, I wasn't sure I wanted to know and, hoping to escape this confession, I interrupted, "I'm going to be traveling a lot and finding a way to work closely with humans, so I'm not sure ye should tell me this secret. Best not to know. Humans might get it out of me." I was coming up with any excuse I could think of to escape knowing.

He laughed in me face, downed his poitín, pointed to me to do the same, which I did, of course, him being me Da and all, and said,

"Oh, humans don't matter. We don't care what ye say to 'em. I'm talking about not passing this on to elementals, especially females."

Well, that was different. I could agree to that, no trouble, so I replied, "That's a different matter. I'd be an eejit not to hear what you've got a mind to say."

That was all the encouragement he needed to continue. "It's something we only tell men when they're ready for handfasting. Before that, they don't need to know as they'll not be in close contact with any females, except their Ma."

Now that I knew where this serious man-to-man was heading, I began to turn red and sweat. We leprechauns stand clear of any sexual, male–female things. He'd never talked to me before about this and now to hear something coming I needed another drink. He saw me ogling the poitín and, no doubt needing some support himself, dipped the ladle back in the brew and topped up our glasses.

"*Sláinte mhaith*," he said, slamming his glass against mine. This means *to your good health* in Irish. Doing so, he was demonstrating some respect for me as a man, an equal.

"*Sláinte mhaith*," I returned, acknowledging his compliment, and downed me drink. Da's poitín was close to 90% proof, so by now neither one of us was entirely sober. I was hoping I'd still be standing when he finally got to the point. Leprechauns, you might have noticed, take a long time getting to the point and have been accused of going everywhere but there. We love a good yarn and like to stretch it out for the fun of it. You could also say that we like to avoid answering certain questions or talking about certain things for certain reasons. All of these things might have been happening as I'm recounting the story.

"To get on with it," Da said and, reaching for another glass of poitín, keeled over. Now, what's a man to do with this state of affairs?

Leprechauns have their pride, so I wasn't going to acknowledge he'd fallen from the drink.

"Thanks be," I said, flinging meself onto the grass to join him. "I didn't think you'd ever sit down and I'm that knackered."

This comment allowed him to save face whilst I, swearing I'd had enough drink, carefully placed me empty glass down. He righted himself with as much dignity as he could muster and, somewhat blurry-eyed, looked at me. His opening was, "Females, you've got to be careful of 'em."

I kept me tongue whilst he continued. "Several hundred years ago, one of our deep lookers decided to study females and how they interacted with lads. We're not talking only young lasses but our mates, and even including older females. Sure, on the surface it looks like they're all docile, sweet and accommodating, implying that our men are the boss, but our deep looker discovered this was a strategy they used to throw us off track. They're really canny. If they *pretend* that they're helpless, they can get us to do the heavy lifting and the jobs they don't want to do. But when they really want something, they drop hints, are extra sweet, and what do you think, we give 'em exactly what they want. How's that for canny?"

Looking me straight in the eye, he waited for a reaction. It hadn't escaped me notice that Aine had some of the qualities he described. I'd also noticed, however, a real backbone and adventurous spirit and, to tell the truth, she hadn't hidden them from me or anyone. Still, there was no sense pointing this out to Da who was not at his best. Could start an argument. Instead I said, "Think you've got a point. What would ye recommend?"

"Ha," he replied, "just where I was going. The deep looker said to keep attentive and give 'em back the same treatment. That means that we're nice and accommodating to 'em and that will outsmart 'em so they'll be nice to us. What do ye think of that!"

To be honest, I thought yer man's argument was a little untidy. However, I liked his recommendation and hoped to always practice being nice and accommodating to Aine. In fact, I'm fairly certain she'd not let me get away with anything else but nothing was to be gained by voicing this. Accordingly, I said to Da, "Thanks for letting me know how to treat the lass and I'll be sure to pass it on to me own lad when the time comes."

He let out a deep sigh of relief to have done his duty by me and ended with, "Right! Think I'll turn in," and off he went hobbling to the door, leaving me to return to me own home.

Bachelor Parties

I suppose you'll want to hear about the handfasting ceremony, what you call the wedding. I'll get to it, by and by, but I'd first like to tell you about the way me mates celebrated me leaving bachelor time.

It's commonly recognized with leprechauns that there are several stages in life. There's the little 'un stage that keeps on till our hormones kick in; the trying stage of sowing our wild oats; the settling stage that I was now entering that called for handfasting and having little 'uns. I was going to stop with me list but I feel you urging me to continue, thus I'll be right nice to you. The fourth stage is for mastering our craft and this is our longest stage and doubles over with the settling stage, just like with humans. Our final, and fifth, stage is being an old one where we pass on to others our wisdom of which, I'm sure you'll agree, leprechauns have a lot.

Most of me mates had already passed into the settling stage, hence were full of advice. I'll let you guess where the best place was to share their knowledge. You're right, the local. But to begin with we had to have a hurling match. You may never have heard of it, even though we've been playing for hundreds, probably thousands, of years—long before your golf and football had been dreamt of. Hurling's the fastest game on Earth and we elementals, being right faster than humans, gave it to you in the first place.

Me mates initially needed to get the word out that they wanted a game between us leprechauns and the goblins. You might wonder, why the goblins? There wouldn't be much of a game with trolls as they're too slow and field faeries would be focusing on play, but goblins would give us men a good match. In fact, they're usually the best, although that's hard to admit. Me mates sent the message through the ethers and leprechauns and goblins came running. Elementals would never put a hurling match second to work, unlike you humans who love to put work ahead of play. More fool you. It was always a good dust up for the community and, when the trolls, trooping faeries, lasses and little 'uns heard, they appeared in a flash. We were holding the match in the field near the ocean, where we'd be dodging the sheep, and this was bound to add good craic to our showing.

I'd best explain our Irish word *craic*. Craic is having a good time and it usually has to do with drinking, eating, music and hanging out with your mates. A good laugh is what you'd call it. It's got nothing at all to do with that drug that humans smoke to relieve miseries. It's hard to put your finger on craic as it slithers away if you try to pin it down. 'Tis an atmosphere that you breathe in that energizes you as much as fresh forest air on a soft spring day. Anyway, about the craic. I can point you in the right direction but I can't take you there.

Now, there's sometimes black craic as well as light craic. Black craic is laughing when something goes awry and elementals enjoy laughing at our misfortunes and those of others as well. We don't see a thing wrong with that, do you? The way we see it, laughter lessens the misfortune.

Anyway, back to me story. Me being the man of the hour and, with Aine watching, I was given the honor of being the one to start. So I grabbed me *camán* (you'd probably call it a stick) and the sliotar (which you'd probably call a ball), and off I set down the field headed for the goblin's goalpost. The leprechauns lined me up with Oisín, our best hurling player, and he was off down the field too and shouting at me to pass the sliotar. But not me, I was wanting to be the hero and continued running, that's when I tripped over a sheep that got in me way. Down I went, flat on me face, and a goblin, quick to see his chance, scooped up the sliotar and off he went back the way I'd come.

Not a good beginning and, no time to nurse me shame, I was after him. Not likely that a leprechaun would ever catch a goblin in a fair race but me mates, being crafty, got their *camán* out as he was racing by. The next moment he was on the dirt and Oisín was headed back me way with the sliotar. I saw me chance and was up and sprinting towards the goblin's end again yelling, "Here. Here. Pass it here." So he did and I saw me chance and hurled the sliotar over the goal. The hero, after all.

Me mates were roaring and carrying me over their heads and the leprechaun crowd went wild for 'tis not so easy scoring a goal against the goblins. This went on for a good time and I would have liked it to have stretched out even longer, but 'twas not to be. The goblins were gathering, waiting their turn to get theirs back. We lined up again and I could see them whispering and knew they were up to something. So it was. One of 'em no sooner got the sliotar than, preceded by a line-up of goblins set to help him, he headed down our end of the field. As we tried to wrest the sliotar away from him, us leprechauns were hooked and blocked and they even herded the sheep towards us to make sure we couldn't get control, until one of 'em swung that sliotar right over the goal.

This isn't exactly the way you humans play the game, but we have our own rules that are fairly near to no rules, except to have great craic. We leprechauns respected the crafty way the goblins had managed their goal and, taking a leaf from their tree, we tried the same thing our next time out. I could tell you the whole game but, coming to the point, I'll say that we leprechauns were not the winner of the match, but we made a good showing and the goblins, acknowledging our play, offered to stand me a pint at the local.

I've been keeping back a bit of a secret that, happily, it's time to share. A notoriety, a famous goblin hurler, had been standing on the side-lines watching the match. Fionn couldn't play as he wasn't a member of our community and this was a locals' game. Anyway, he cheered on the goblins and they rallied to see him there and, when they won, they ran to him in celebration. The goblins were over the moon that Fionn, their goblin hero, had witnessed their victory over the leprechauns. You'll never guess whose friend he was. Aye, yours truly. Fionn and I knew each other from wandering the road and we were part of the same group of elementals interested in working with humans. The local goblins naturally assumed he was there for them, and so he was, but Fionn was also there to celebrate me.

He'd been that proud of me, that he said to the other goblins, "Mates, you're the clear victors, but it's yer man's time (pointing to me) and I'm sure you'd like to be invited to the handfasting celebrations as they're great craic. Let's treat ALL the leprechaun lads to a round at the local and that'll stand us in good stead to be invited to the handfasting."

How could they say 'naw' when their hero was asking? What they didn't see was Fionn winking at me out of the corner of his eye signaling, clear as day, that he'd not let on he knew me. This would be a double clever trick. Firstly, Fionn tricked his fellow goblins and, secondly, he tricked me leprechaun friends at the same time. Only him and me would be enjoying the craic in this caper. Now, we'd get to see if he could pull it off in front of goblins and leprechauns, both experts at such shenanigans.

Off we went to the local. Leprechauns don't need to be invited twice if it means we'll be getting something free. The goblins were a bit reluctant as they figured something strange had just happened but they couldn't figure out the mischief. Still, they fell in and were soon jockeying for position on who'd get to sit beside Fionn. In their eagerness, they were pushing and shoving each other into humans in the pub and, much to the human's chagrin, their beer was slopping over the floor. The bartender was not keen on all the 'accidents' and called out to more than a few of them, "Keep your drink in your glass, man."

These comments naturally spurred two goblins into a competition to see who could get a human to make the grandest slop. Leprechauns and goblins set up bets on which goblin would win and the poor human bloke didn't stand a chance. "Push his arm to the left whilst I push his foot to the right," said the one.

"You push the arm and I'll take the foot," countered the other, wanting to stay clear of any slop coming his way.

"'Twas me idea originally," retorted the one.

"But I'm the oldest and you'd best mind that," retaliated the second, pushing on the human's leg to put his plan into action.

"Dónal, git over here and lend a hand," the first yells at the largest goblin on the sidelines.

Whilst Dónal did what he was bid, the second goblin hollered to his son, "Fergus, help your ole Da."

And so it went until all the goblins had made a line on one side or t'other. The human was fair rocking from side to side turning green in the face and was getting strange looks from the bartender and his mates when the first goblin group gave a great heave and over he toppled, drink an' all.

"That's it for the night, lad," said the bartender, brooking no guff, whilst the lad's mates hoisted him to his feet and marched him out. The night out for them was a fair mess, but a good game for us leprechauns, and for me, especially, as I'd bet on the first goblin. Getting gold at me bachelor was a good luck charm to be ready for handfasting. The bachelor night with me mates was a grand success with lots of Guinness drunk and games played. Fionn stayed till the end to witness it all and was sure to report back to our wandering group, which would give much joy to them too.

By now, me and Aine had been courting a year. I've told you about me bachelor party; however, the event for lasses is quite different. No men are allowed, thus it's hard to know exactly what happens. For a fact, what I do know is that the lass who's to be handfasted is kept in isolation with the older women for a week before the ceremony. That said, sometimes us leprechauns ask a goblin, them being crafty like us, to discover what happened at the lasses' event.

We've an enterprising young goblin, Declan, who's started up a business to go to the cottage where the young lasses to be handfasted are kept in isolation with the older women. Peeping any way he was able, he would see and hear what transpired and then report back to us leprechauns. You might wonder why we never asked another leprechaun. That would be too suspicious. The older women would be looking out for us to do that but goblins are noted for going wherever they want, whenever they want, so they wouldn't be questioned. Also, goblins have exceptional hearing and could hear conversations through the walls. Not that it would come to that, as they've also got great sight, and could peer through a small chink in a wall. I was eager to receive as much information as possible, therefore I hired Declan. After all, leprechauns know that information is power.

Returning from the spying mission, this is what Declan reported. According to him, the older women started the week's handfasting preparation with the physical. Aine had already learned how to sew, cook and milk the coos when she was younger. However, during the week, the matriarchs, who were considered the experts in every female discipline, gave her further training. They critiqued her work till she got as good as she was ever going to get. Next, she needed to learn how to please her mate, when to speak, what to say and how to say it in a way both to keep the peace and to still keep her authority.

Finally, the lass received the final touches. There was an ole crone whose job it was to study each man in the village to see what kind of a character he had. She started looking when the lad was just a little 'un and followed him as he grew. The finale of the week was when the crone delivered her findings to the women. When Declan got to this part of his account, he looked up at me with a mad twinkle in his eye. Not a look to inspire confidence and, drawing out the suspense, he told me what the crone said.

"Tis not easy to predict anything about that man whom you've chosen," she began. "He's never played by our rules (Declan paused to increase me anxiety), at least the rules we've had till now. Even as a little 'un, he held himself back from the rest and was always watching everyone. Made a lot of us uncomfortable, it did. Sure, he was not disobedient. We watched to see if he'd mind his Ma, as well as his Da, as it's a known fact that if he didn't mind his Ma, he'd be a bad bet as a mate for a lass. (Longer pause) But he did mind his Ma. She only needed to ask him to do something and he'd hop to it. However, he wasn't studying his Da's work to learn his craft, unlike the younger lad. (Pause) He'd do it if his Da asked him, but not otherwise."

Declan said that me lass's Ma interrupted the crone to ask, "Did he play with other young 'uns his age?"

To which the crone answered, "He did and, strange though it be, they often looked to him to be the leader."

"Why do you say, 'tis strange'?" asked Aine's Ma, wanting to make sure there was no aberration in me character.

"Well, he's not the biggest so he can't lead by brawn and he's not pushing himself to be noticed like some who want to lead. Additionally, he's not got the most famous ancestors, thus his family lines won't help him."

"That's a lot of what's he's not got; what *has* he got?" asked me lass's Ma. (At this point, me goblin hire looked at me with a strange *gotcha* grin on his face.)

"That's what's strange," commented the crone, puzzled. "If I were pushed to remark, I'd state he's more of a scholar. Since a young 'un, he's liked to visit the Old Ones and that's not normal. He visits leprechauns doing various crafts rather than learning his Da's craft. He also likes to wander far from home and brings back all sorts of new ideas to our community (long pause, holding the breath) like partnering with humans. That's really not normal."

"However," Declan said, interrupting his account, "the lass's Ma was getting quite worked up listening to the negative recounting of your character but not half as worked up as your Ma, who jumped to your defense.

"I'm not saying that your facts aren't right, 'cos they are," she exclaimed, "but I take offense at you saying me lad's not normal. He's a good leprechaun and proud of his family and community. If he's doing something a bit different, it could be he's the founder of a new way, maybe a new craft. That's why his mates treat him like a leader."

Declan, in his next aside, said, "Aine was fair beaming to hear you defended by your Ma. She's not allowed to speak as that's the way in these women pre-handfasting gatherings where only the older ones can speak. She was only meant to listen. In fact, no one wanted to speak against the crone and you could see them sitting with pursed lips and hands tucked under aprons, hoping peace would be maintained. It depended on the crone's next words and there was a long pause, as she digested what your Ma had said. All held their breaths as the silence stretched."

As Declan spoke, he drew out the pause for emphasis, creating a good deal of tension for this poor suffering leprechaun. According to Declan, the crone finally said, "I'd not thought of that. A new craft would be a good idea, sure it would."

"Aye," everyone agreed, letting out their breaths. Even if leprechauns are traditional, they love their crafts and any talk of creating a new one is a cause for celebration.

Declan's been on many of these listening-ins and has got to know what's customary and what's notably different. Goblins love different things happening. It's food for them and his ears perked up to hear the next words addressed by the crone to me lass.

"It's not usual that I'd dissect a lass's character but your courting with your man has been everything but usual."

"That's when a grand silence descended and a tense breathless pause ensued," said Declan. "Taking a good look through the small gap in the wall, I saw all the females, except for the two Mas, looking at their hands. Seems like the two Mas were united in disapproval for they glared at the crone, daring her to cast aspersions on your lass's character."

The crone, undaunted, continued. "Not to worry that I'd attack a lass before her handfasting. I was only commenting that you've been an unusual lass, Aine. You'd not suit a usual lad in our community, hence you've been right crafty and made a fine choice, given your options. I wish you well, as we all do here."

"So," said Declan, "there were smiles and laughter all round as everyone congratulated your lass at being crafty enough to get the only lad that would have her." Hearing Declan's account, I realized that the ole crone had put her words in such a way that the others could celebrate me lass being crafty. That was kindly.

Me goblin hire got bored at that point and, feeling he'd earned his gold, left. So I can't say what happened next. All I know is that I wasn't to see me lass until our handfasting day.

Handfasting and Beltane

The day dawned lovely. Most elementals want to have their handfasting in spring as that's the most auspicious time, when the Earth sings of love and beauty and seeds sprout into young plants. Animals, birds and all nature mates in spring and we elementals follow the harmony of the seasons.

Me lass and I were having our handfasting that special May day that we refer to as Beltane. Do you know about Beltane? You might think you do, but do you know how elementals celebrate? I think you don't. Formerly, we were the ones who gave humans the idea to celebrate the turning of the seasons and we did that so far back in your history that you can't even recall it. I'll explain how we do it, shall I?

You may be wondering why Aine and me would have chosen Beltane for the handfasting. All elementals want May Day, for it's a celebration of fertility and new growth and we want that ritual to bless our handfasting and living together years. As we all want that day, there were many other couples, not all leprechauns, lined up for the handfasting too. So, there was a wee bit of competition about who'd get the biggest thorn bush for their event. The trick was to get out early, stake your bush, and then leave a mate to look after it whilst you went to get beautified. The leprechauns would be out for theirs; the goblins for theirs; the trolls for theirs… you get the picture. We'd all be after a hawthorn although, if stuck, you could accept a rowan but you wouldn't get the same luck that way, so it wasn't the best choice.

Therefore, early in the morning before the sun rose, I had staked out a large thorn tree and me best mate from the road, Shamus, was supposed to relieve me so I could leave and get ready. But where was he? And who do you think showed up next? Me goblin hire.

"What are you doing here," says I. "I've staked this thorn tree for me handfasting this day."

"And where's your mate who's to mind the bush?" says Declan, looking crafty.

"He'll be here anytime," replies me, starting to wonder.

"Will he now?" asks Declan, smirking.

"Will he not?" says I, getting worried.

"I wouldn't be reckoning he would," says he. "Him, not being a local, he doesn't know his way around here."

"And where would he be?" asks I, getting irritated.

"Other side of the village by now, I reckon," laughs he.

"And why's he there?" probes me, studying me nails and trying to be nonchalant.

"Think he overheard me say to one of me mates that you'd gone there instead of coming here."

Declan had me, for sure. Leprechauns love to negotiate to make the best deal but this couldn't happen that day and didn't he know it. "What's the fee?" asks I, wanting instead to give him one to the stomach.

"I was going to say two gold pieces but now I'll say three," retorts he, angry that I wasn't a good loser.

"How do you know I won't get you back after me handfasting celebration?" asks I, still not ready to concede defeat.

"I'll be unavailable till the fire tonight when you'll need to forget your ill will to me," replies he, smiling.

"I hand it to you. You've got me good," I acknowledged, in an attempt at humor, which wasn't easy as leprechauns don't part easily from their gold. Wasn't he the grand strategist! He'd have made a great leprechaun.

"For that, me friend," says Declan, generously, "you can have the bush for two gold pieces and I'll stay here and watch it till your wandering leprechaun friend makes it here."

"Done," says I, spitting on me hand and extending it to close the deal.

"Done," he replied, spitting on his hand and shaking mine.

That very moment, Shamus appeared and, at that exact instant, that rogue Declan disappeared.

None the wiser, Shamus apologizing for his tardiness, said, "Sorry I'm late but I thought it was a different thorn." Obviously, he wasn't going to mention that he'd been done by a goblin and I wasn't going to mention it either. We leprechauns like to keep our pride.

"No harm done," replied I, generously, and went immediately to the cottage to look after me own handfasting preparations.

Since I was a bachelor and living alone, the cottage had got into a bit of a state with clothes lying here and there, not to mention dirty this and that. What I'm saying is that it needed a spring-cleaning before Aine came. What's a man to do? I sent a message through the ethers to me Ma for help. It wasn't a minute before she walked in the door carrying broom, mop, pail, soap, rags and the like. Obviously, she had it all prepared and was only waiting for the signal to come.

"Out now," she said, shuffling me through the door. "Go gather spring flowers for the bed and table."

I didn't need to be told twice and headed for the gorse. We elementals have got a saying: 'Love will be in fashion as long as the gorse is in bloom.' Gorse blooms for eons so I wanted it to represent me love for Aine. Also, we use gorse in our Beltane ceremonies to light the fire. There being gorse everywhere, there was no shortage of where to look. I got bundles of it and made certain to gather purple heather and white hawthorn for added color. A wise lad knows what pleases a lass and I was up to doing that to get off on the right foot.

By the time I returned to the cottage, Ma had it looking bright and cheery. Taking the flowers, she put them on the door and table and, pulling the blooms off the sweet-smelling May bush, she strewed them on the bed. She was making everything as welcoming as could be and ensuring that Aine would feel part of our family right away. Ma is wise that way and, when she was handfasted, she'd learned this from me Da's Ma. She'd even cleaned me best green coat and did what she could with me hat, which had seen some hard days wandering the road.

I dressed in a hurry and, taking one last glance at me cottage, bid farewell to me bachelor time. Out the door I went and onto the lane where me mates waited to walk me to the thorn. Cheers went up and I could see that some might have had a nip of poitín to set up for the special day. Not to worry, I'd not had a drop. Me best mate, Shamus, put a wreath of May bush flowers round me neck and cheered some more. All in good fun, however he'd not thought to remove the thorns. Still, I wasn't about to moan when he was trying hard to fit in with the locals. Instead, I hoisted the wreath under the collar of me coat so as not to pierce me jugular on this special day. Sure I knew there'd be lots of hugging and I didn't want to risk injury.

Giving the leprechaun community a chance to gather, we made a grand procession on our way to the thorn. The May bush was festooned with ribbons and gold hurling balls and 'twas clear the folks had had a grand time decorating it. I was asked to stand by the tree where I waited for the lass. I saw her coming over the hill and was astonished by her. May flowers were woven through Aine's black hair and she was carrying a spring bouquet but what was truly astonishing was that she was wearing white, like a human woman would wear at her wedding. Normally, our women would wear green for their handfasting but here she was breaking with tradition yet again. It was clear to me and to the others that, given me predisposition in wanting to work with humans, Aine was advertising her support of me. What courage she had. I was that proud of her.

Up she comes so close I could see her fair skin and freckles glistening. Made me knees go weak. One of our leprechaun Old Ones got out the ribbons to do the handfasting and together we extended our hands and touched. Soft skin she had, but I didn't have time to think on that as the Old One got the ribbon too tight, leaving us to loosen it before losing our circulation. This caused quite a stir 'cos the community evidently thought we'd had last-minute doubts and were trying to get clear of each other.

Aine and I, realizing this, burst out laughing, whilst I turned to the Old One and said, "Cut us loose, man. Our hands are turning blue."

At me words, everyone understood what had occurred and hooted in glee at the same moment that Shamus cried, "Get them now before they're free." Everyone sprang to embrace us whilst we were still bound together. It's not usual that males and females touch, hence the females were hugging her and the males were thumping me.

When we finally disentangled ourselves, we were whisked off to the largest barn in our community where a great feed was set up for our partaking. The handfasting was a grand affair and the mead flowed freely. We'll take Guinness if there's nothing else, but we prefer mead, made from the honey of our little friends, the bees. There was plenty of brown bread and butter and honey. Plenty of milk and cream. And fiddlers, pipes, drum and squeeze box played cheery tunes and everyone was dancing. Most of the community was happy about our marriage 'cos they'd been worried about both the lass and me, thinking that we'd be lost from the community because of our strange ideas and ways.

The festivities broke up as evening approached for we all wanted to get to the fire to celebrate the second part of Beltane. You need a big fire to get rid of the old and bring in the new and fire's the fastest, most powerful, element to burn away the old. On Beltane, our tradition is to clean our cottages and put on our best clothes as we want to look our best for the night. We do that to be as attractive as possible for the evening's festivities. Why? Because it's on Beltane that we can do whatever we want and be excused the next day. This means that, if an elf fancies a leprechaun and that leprechaun fancies the elf, they can join up for the evening with no questions asked, whereas usually we elementals stick tightly to our clans in such things. Even the gossips are not to say a thing later and no one will comment on what they've been up to either.

It's also a time when, if your coo is ailing, you walk it up to the fire and receive a blessing. The healing works for us too. Elementals are seldom ill, not even in old age, but if we've mis-stepped and hurt our foot, or if that ruddy coo stepped on it, we can smoke our foot over the sacred fire to cure it. I can just hear you humans doubting and the main problem with curing your own aches and pains is that you disbelieve it will work. We elementals don't have this problem. We know it works, so it does.

Which brings me to another thing we do on Beltane. That's to forget someone's ill will. Maybe you've spoken ill of someone or even twisted the truth a wee bit to make yourself look grand at another's expense. Beltane will fix it. You wait till the fire's blazing and then, taking a smoking branch, high thee hence to the injured party and give it to him. He takes the branch with good will and circles you with it and the smoke burns away the ill will. Now, if by chance, that one has done you a bad turn too, he gives the branch back to you and you circle him with it, doing the same. Then, together you take the branch back to the fire. So, there's a lot of traveling branches and forgetting and forgiving on Beltane. This way, we keep a peaceful community during the year.

All the elementals in our community gathered at the one fire as we had a small enough village that we could do this. And it was time for the traditional contest where the men saw who could leap the highest over the fire. It was considered a sign of prowess and the man who won would be the most sought out for the evening by the lasses. Now, leprechauns are a bit stocky and not at all good at this, therefore we weren't expected to do well. The goblins and even field faeries are generally the winners and this is all in good sport and no one minds.

However, sometimes us leprechauns get to thinking about how to compete better and this was one of those times. Seems like some of the young 'uns, who'd been listening to me yarns about new human sports, had decided to set me up trying one. They'd cut a long branch of rowan, stripped off the side branches, and decorated it with ribbons and some bells borrowed off a coo. Clutching the branch, they thrust it at me, urging me to demonstrate the human sport of pole vaulting.

I'm not much into athletics and have never tried anything close to this and was not eager to try on me handfasting night with the whole community gawking. Thus, I didn't take the pole and said, "C'mon, one o' you young 'uns. Give it a go!"

"You're the expert. Show us how it's done," the young 'uns insisted.

One young leprechaun grabbed the pole, called everyone to attention by pointing at me, and announced, "Yer man here in celebration for his handfasting will demonstrate the new sport of stick jumping over the fire."

Having neatly escaped having me jugular pieced earlier by the wreath of thorns, I was now in danger of having my buttocks or worse roasted on my handfasting night. Aine's eyes were glued to me and even the goblins were cheering. I especially noted Declan, to whom I owed two gold pieces, taking delight at the situation and cheering me on.

Nothing to be done. To save face, I'd best brave it out. Trying to remember what I'd heard about the game, I gripped the end of the pole and, trying not to get the ribbons caught in me teeth, ran at the fire and leapt. Now, I wouldn't be saying there was anything graceful in the action but, somehow, I made it across without being singed and all hailed the attempt. Many of the young 'uns struggled to grab the pole from me hands, something I willingly relinquished, and started throwing themselves across the fire on the pole, competing to see who could jump the highest. None beat the goblins who were the clear winners of the competition, but it was all great craic.

Accordingly, the evening progressed and odd couples started to depart. I caught Aine glancing up at me and wasn't she blushing as she picked up me thoughts. I said goodbye to me mates, who stuffed gold coins into me hand to celebrate the handfasting, and was walking over to me lass when Declan grabbed me arm.

"Here's the gold you were promised," I said, giving him the two gold coins.

"Not to worry about the gold," he replied, giving me the gold back. "When ye go back on the road, let me know." With those words, he turned and sauntered off, leaving me hanging.

I'll cut me story short now as we don't go into any more personal stuff. Let's just say that

Aine and I went to live in Crumpaun Cottage. She and I wanted to have a family right away but we weren't that lucky. I felt old friends in the power nodes calling me to continue the work we'd started and, when I told Aine, she encouraged me to join them. She was happy to stay behind, even though there weren't any young 'uns yet, for she wanted to establish herself in the cottage and get things in order. Also, she could visit me family as well as her own and show the community in Keel that she was a respectable leprechaun.

Working with Humans

All the elementals who wanted to work with humans were being called to Uisneah, one of the royal sites of Ireland, in the center of the island, where they would form a new group. We're talking about leprechauns, trolls, goblins, elves, field faeries and more, so finding a way of working together was a brand new happening in our elemental world. I was getting everything I wanted in life. I was grateful for the good fortune with me lass and community in Keel and also being able to work with humans in the wider world. But, it was time to leave.

I packed up the goods I'd need on the road for sleeping out in all weather with scanty rations. First, you need sturdy shoes and me Da made the best so that was the easiest thing to come by. Next, there was a new human invention—a Macintosh rain jacket—which was perfect for inclement weather but sweltering on a summer's day. Nevertheless, as autumn was upon us, I was prepared because, under the rain jacket, I had me own jacket. I'd never part with that or me brown wool trousers. Aine had knitted me a lovely woolly jumper and, as I stuffed it in me pack for cool nights, she beamed with pride.

I only just finished packing when I heard a knock on the door. Opening it, I saw Declan standing on the step with a pack on his back.

"I'm ready to go," says he. "What's keeping ye?"

"Going where?" says I, pretending I'd no idea what he was talking about.

"Uisneah, of course. I've been waiting forever and now the time's come. Thought we could saunter along together and you could fill me in on the group before we get there."

Wasn't that enterprising of him to think he'd get a leg up from the master. You had to respect his initiative. That was the start of how I ended up taking a goblin under me wing.

"Right. Wait outside whilst I part with me lass and we'll walk a piece together." Shutting the door, I turned around to say goodbye and saw Aine holding two loaves of brown bread, honey and butter for me to take.

"That will keep you going," she announced, her eyes glistening with unshed tears. She was putting on a brave face and I was relieved that she didn't ask when I'd be back, for I hadn't a clue.

"Thank ye, lass," says I, giving her a big hug and opening the door before I, too, waxed weepy.

"Off we go then, Declan," I said, putting on me deepest male voice, making him know who was the senior of the two. As he fell in beside me, keeping back a bit, thus having proved me point, I mellowed.

"Why do ye want to partner with humans?" I inquired, curious.

"I've been listening to your stories and it sounds exciting, something new. 'Tis boring in Keel," he replied.

"'Tis hard work and that's a fact," I remarked, making sure he didn't think he was going on holiday.

"I'm not afraid of work. I made me listening-in business a success, didn't I? But now I've done it, I'm looking for something more meaningful."

"Them's high words," I answered, trying to decipher what he was saying. Leprechauns, unlike goblins, are very practical and I wanted to get him out of the clouds and onto the ground.

Color rose to his cheeks and Declan glanced away as he replied, "It might sound ungoblin-like but I'm not interested in playing jokes on folks. I don't really fit in the goblin community. I feel more drawn to what your mixed group of elementals are doing."

That was quite an admission to one who wasn't even of his clan. "None of us working with humans feel we fit in with the traditions of our clan, so you'll fit in fine," I replied, clapping him on the back. However, I couldn't help adding a note of reality. "Even so, you're young still and you'll be surprised how fondly you think of home and Keel after being on the road awhile."

Having got ourselves sorted, we headed for Uisneah. Uisneah is sacred for both leprechauns and humans, hence it was a perfect place for the two groups to meet. To make it clear, many of the humans came in their etheric not their physical bodies. These humans were people like Rudolf Steiner and other wise ones who wanted to work with elementals. The humans included many bards, healers and hedge teachers who knew a lot of the old lore in Ireland. Surprisingly, there were also a few females as well as males who came not only from Ireland but also from around Europe.

On me own behalf, I have to say that me role was not insignificant for I was already a way-shower for many others, especially for those of the leprechaun race. Twelve humans were designated to work with each of the twelve elemental clans and I was named as the head of the leprechaun group. A high king of the elves had sent out his forest elves to find out more about our group and, hearing their report, he joined us himself. One of the goblin heads was in our group but, at this point, he wasn't given too much power. Knowing the mischievous reputation of goblins, the other elemental clans were watching to see if he intended to shake up our process. Because of this decision and now that I'd got to know Declan better, I was beginning to see me prejudices as unfair. It's hard to kick a prejudice and even harder to get others to kick theirs, when they've not had the positive experience I've had. Observing Declan watching the proceedings and how he placed himself halfway between the goblins and the leprechauns, I knew he was biding his time to see which way the wind blew. He was a smart one.

A few trolls and their head came down from Scandinavia and Norway specially to connect with us. In fact, various kinds of gnomes and elementals who were forming their own groups in Europe had come to introduce themselves and to learn more about our organization. They were more observers and, in turn, we were invited to be observers for their circles in Europe.

Humans and elementals from all these countries, clans and backgrounds came together to determine the best way to work together. We discovered that, when we got right down to it, both our elemental and human representatives wanted to help the natural world, which had been suffering since the coming of the industrial age. We knew that partnering with each other was the way to do it because each of us had talents that were needed by the other.

For instance, humans manifest what they want in the material world through their will; however, they are unconscious of how their thoughts and feelings affect their physical world. Elementals, on the other hand, living in the higher astral world, know how our thoughts and feelings create form, not only in our realm, but in all realms, but they don't have a strong enough will to change the physical realm without human help.

After we got to know each other and appointed the heads of each clan, it was time for each elemental and human to choose a partner with whom to work. Steiner and I chose each other as we'd already formed a bond during our earlier meetings. Working with elementals was not his only work but it was part of it. Besides, I was not the only one he worked with as he had a calling to work with elementals from all clans. Which brings me to me next point, which is that I couldn't fail to notice that I, too, was attracting elementals from all clans. So Steiner and me, even in that way, we had this similar bond.

He decided to teach humans about the importance of working with elementals through writing books and talks. In those, he spoke about our function and how, without elementals, there'd be no rocks, trees, plants, water—nothing, in fact, as we are the builders of form in the world. Watching him, I made the decision to travel around the Earth to meet elementals and to tell them about humans that wanted to co-create with us to make a beautiful and healthy world. Steiner and I worked well together; he sent me humans and I sent him elementals.

Elementals can travel in space and time, therefore 'twas easy to go to other countries just by thinking about it. Also, in the astral world, beings communicate with telepathy, hence it wasn't a problem being understood in various languages—a problem that you humans run up against in the physical world. What was difficult was getting used to different habits and eating uncommon foods. Leprechauns are fairly traditional with such things and, I'll admit, this was a stretch for me. For instance, that fluffy French and Italian stuff they call bread is terrible compared to our Irish soda bread with oats, which is real food with substance. One of the best things, on the other hand, was sampling the various kinds of drink and

I was sure to take our poitín to give 'em a sample. 'Twas grand to try their honey too and for them to try our Irish honey.

Everywhere I traveled, I found elementals who were interested in joining our group to partner with humans. I was delighted when I attracted elementals from diverse clans and usually it was the young 'uns. More and more, I discovered that the way to do this was to respect the traditions of these diverse cultures and to try to fit in. So, in Hawaii, I wore leis and grass skirts; in America, I was off to the west in tipis, braving a sweat lodge; and, in Africa, I was often down to a loincloth that caused fearful burns to me delicate skin.

Elementals prefer living in the country and are often closer to indigenous rather than modern city folk, as indigenous peoples are closer to the Earth. Consequently, this is where I often found me converts. Steiner, on the other hand, was good at pulling in elementals and humans from the cities and gradually they started joining together with our country folk.

You may be wondering if I ever got back to Keel and me home. Sure I did, but not as often as I liked. Time in our elemental world is not the same as human time and I knew Steiner didn't have as many years for his task as I had for mine. Therefore, I wondered, as he got older, who'd replace him. As it happened, he got fewer years than I'd hoped but we'd done a good job of starting up elemental and human groups before his end came. By that time, the whole group was much larger and stronger and each elemental and human was committed.

After he passed, I went home for a good long rest. I still did forays into the world to teach the young 'uns and to support those groups that were established but it wasn't as tough as the start-up time. It was more the steady growing time. I'd become a bit of a leader and, as a result, elementals from other parts of Ireland and even other countries would often knock on me door. Me lass Aine would always welcome them nicely and give them tea and cake. So, 'twas a good life having both a home and meaningful work.

I suppose the great beings who oversee us didn't want me to get set in me ways as I began to sense another change coming. Ahhh, sure, the world had been changing aplenty as it was but I mean something specifically in the work between humans and elementals. That's when, decades after Steiner's passing, another human partner came to Crumpaun Cottage and simply walked in the door. Tanis it was. She was a female and a cross between city and country lass and young enough to give me many years of partnering. She had mystical gifts, being able to hear everything I had to teach her, and wasn't so set in her ways that she couldn't be swayed to work on our behalf. In other words, perfect. Anyway, I've no reason to re-tell the story of our meeting as it's told in our first book, *Summer with the Leprechauns*, which we wrote together, not to mention all the other books we've done.

I could tell you about me home life when I was back living in the cottage in Keel, but me lass has got a different idea. Aine's made it clear that she wants to record her story now and, as she's in charge of the home, she claims she's the expert on the next part of the story. Can't say as how I blame her for wanting to get in on the fun. She's been seeing me enjoying recounting me story and she wants to give it a go. Go easy on her, as it's her first time.

It's not hard to describe me sweet lass. She's not quite as tall as me and she's got the brightest blues eyes and fair skin nicely sprinkled with freckles and her glossy black hair falls to her waist. If you're wondering about her dress, I'd have to say that, lately, she's gone peculiar in that area for that Tanis has contaminated her with modern human fashion ideas. Aine's cast aside her traditional jacket and skirt for *trousers*. Can ye imagine?

Aine was dead keen to tell her story and, after Lloyd waved goodbye, she jumped right in.

The Leprechaun Lass's Story

The reason I want to speak with you is that Himself (meaning Lloyd) wouldn't get the woman's story right and it's important to set the record straight about the similarities and differences in the roles that men and women have in the human and leprechaun worlds. Unlike in your human realm, elemental men and women have different roles. We don't usually speak together about our different roles, although yer man and I talk among ourselves more than other couples we know in the leprechaun community. He regards me mind as a good fountain of information, perception and good sense. Still, talking to Himself isn't the same as speaking to another female.

In your faerie stories, there are only male leprechauns and you'd think there were no females at all and that's a mistake. It's true that in our leprechaun society the men do the talking and play their clever games on humans. If you ever saw a female leprechaun, you might think it was a brownie or something similar as we're often about the same size and build. I, for instance, come to the top of me man's heart, which is about three and a half feet in human terms, but he's tall for a leprechaun and we're both a bit stocky, but in a good way, mind. What's more, in the ole days, leprechaun and brownie women didn't dress all that different. At that time, we women wore long skirts down to our ankles and an apron and sometimes a bit of a flowered blouse. If we were getting dressed up for a handfasting or special event, we'd wear a close-fitting little jacket and a belt with a nice buckle. We'd even have buckles on our shoes.

Women don't go out that much but stay home and look after the little 'uns and, when we do get together, women most often gossip, probably about our men. Anyway, from a young age, I've been uncomfortable with other females as many of me interests are different. However, I do try to fit in. As Himself told you, it did take courage to decide to marry him because we elementals can see the path of someone's journey before they even start it. We can see the future as clearly as the present. He'd come to a fork in the road and he could have decided to stay as a cobbler in the village but I could see that wasn't likely his choice.

I, also, could have decided to assume a traditional female role in the village but it would have squashed me. I was only really happy wandering the hills and learning from the wind and natural elements. Elementals can hear what's being said on the wind and it tells us what's happening in other places in the world. This is one of the ways we pick up information. You humans could listen to the wind, if you wanted to, and you'd be hearing the same stories.

We're remote on Achill but I'd been hearing from the wind what was happening in the rest of Ireland and even on the continent. I'd heard about the wars and what we Irish call the famine. We elementals were struck by the famine too. We take the essence out of food and 'twas not easy getting oats for stiraway. That's what we elementals call porridge and it's a staple food for us. Humans were unable to put out any food for elementals at that time as they had little enough and we didn't want to take any from them either, them being in such dire straits and dying in droves. Hence, we were hungry too. You may think there was only one famine, but there was a second one in the late 1870s, by your reckoning, and that's the famine I'm referring to. You call it the mini-famine but there was nothin' mini about it in the west of Ireland where we lived. We called it the *Gorta Beag*—the small hunger, but small only by comparison with the big one, *Gorta Mór.*

And we were famished for good craic as well. Good craic, in case you don't know, is laughing, singing, dancing and joking, and craic's as much food to us as actual food. In those days, there was no good craic to be had and we were fading from the lack of that as much as from anything else. The women wore darker, more somber clothes and not their red vests and green skirts. They wore more brown and even black as if they were in mourning with the humans. This was a sad sight to see and sad for us to live through.

Although I was still young to get married, it was clear to me that, if I couldn't find a man to suit, I'd end up the local match-maker. That's not a job I wanted. I wanted to have a family, companionship, and not be living on me own. Even though it might look like I wanted to be on me own, as I was wandering the hills, it was only so I could have a bit of excitement and listen to the wind. If I was with the gossiping and chatty women in the village, I couldn't listen to the wind.

The wind was me teacher, educating me about humans and how you and elementals lived in other places in the world. You read books to learn history but, in earlier days, you had oral teachings from the bards and hedge teachers who passed history down through your generations. But where do you think they got this oral history and the ability to remember it all? They listened to the wind. Very seldom would a human put what I'm saying into words. Instead, you'd say something like 'a little bird told me', which is the same thing as what I'm telling you.

Elementals can also learn other languages by listening to the wind. However, that's not necessary for elementals 'cos we speak telepathic to each other. Another way elementals pick up information is from water sprites who live in healing and sacred wells. Have you ever noticed that some water is healing and some not? You might wonder why that is. It's because of the water sprites who live in the water. They're dedicated to healing and love to bless the animals, elementals, and even humans that come to their waters.

Sometimes I'd go and sit by a pond or walk by the ocean where I could listen to the great ones in the ocean who were talking about what was happening in the world. The little sprites would be telling the same stories as the big ones 'cos they are all connected by the element of water. In the same way, the little elementals of the air—sylphs we call 'em—can tell the same stories as the big ones 'cos they're all joined by the element of air. The big ones tell the story louder and more thoroughly. They don't only drop a hint but give the whole of it.

The land shares its stories as well. In Keel, if you go up to the bog where the peat is, you can hear what the land says about the people who lived there, even thousands of years ago. When I was a young 'un, I'd sometimes walk up near Slievemore and there'd still be people living there. Humans abandoned Slievemore after the famine. However, there are still elementals living out there now.

Through the water, air and land elementals, I was picking up information about the unpleasant changes in the world that were affecting elementals. This made me think that I might have to go on the road like yer man. But I didn't want to do it. I wanted to stay in the village to have a home and family. I was enough of a leprechaun to be thinking like that and not one of them forest elves that are good at wandering. Did you know that leprechaun feet, compared to those of the elves, are bigger in relation to our bodies, hence we're more grounded. Thus, when yer man returned from wandering and showed an interest in me, I got a better option. Himself had already met that human, Rudolf Steiner, and they already had a relationship, so I knew all I was inheriting by accepting yer man. But he was the most exciting mate I'd likely find and he felt the same way about me. Leprechauns like to mate with leprechauns. We're not into mixing our clans if you're an elemental.

After we got handfasted, I stayed at home and he went on the road. That suited me fine. Yer man had already moved into the cottage before I knew him. At that time, there was one woman—a human that is—living in Crumpaun Cottage with me. She had one room as her bedroom and Himself and I had another and the woman and us shared the sitting room and kitchen. I made it quite comfortable. I think she could probably feel me around but it was all agreeable between the two of us. Sometimes a young nephew of hers would visit and he'd stay in the room with us leprechauns. Perhaps he'd see me as well but we all got along fine. There didn't seem to be any problems.

One of the more attractive things about Himself, from me point of view, was that he wanted to settle in the village and be part of the leprechaun community. We didn't have little 'uns for a while and it wouldn't have been the right thing. I had to get used to living on me own when he wasn't around, which was most of the time. Besides, I needed to learn how to fit in with the other mated women. There are secrets that mated women have that unmated women don't, so the two groups don't mingle.

The mated women now accepted me better than they had before me handfasting. They were good at getting secrets out of me about what Himself was doing and who he was working with and what was happening. They didn't listen to the wind like I did. They were busy talking among themselves and trading their own wind. I could've told 'em stories from me own point of view but they wouldn't respect the information as much as if I said it had come from Himself. I had to let on that I was picking up information by overhearing him nattering with other men and not say that he was actually talking to me. They'd have been in an uproar if they knew that me and Himself sat and talked in an evening by the fire and that he'd tell me stuff as if I were a man. This is not the way with men and women—not if you're a leprechaun, anyway.

I know that humans would like to know about our 'private' life, but all I'll say is that we arrange conception in the same way humans do. Physically I mean… ohhhh, there I go blushing. Now, to change the topic, elementals have a lot more power to decide what kind of child they want than human females have. I could decide what kind of boys I wanted. I wanted a girl too but yer man's energy was so strong that 'twas a given that I'd have all boys. All leprechaun women want a little lass to raise and teach and to help out around the home. Because male and female roles are very different, I'd me hands full with three males and no lass to assist.

Me first one came, then the second. When Tanis was living in our cottage in 1985, she said that the boys looked about five and eight but actually they were much older than that. They would have been about twenty human years old at that time, even if they didn't look that way to humans. Because we're very long-lived—even hundreds of years—our children stay children for a long time.

Mind, I wasn't talking to humans. Tanis thought I was a bit silly when she met me and I can't say I'm pleased being thought of that way, so now I'm setting the story straight. Truth be told,

I wouldn't talk with her then as I didn't feel comfortable talking with a human. That would have been still another step away from the leprechaun ways of doing things. Still, I was overhearing the conversations that Himself and Tanis were having but me main focus was trying to keep me home together with the two young 'uns.

In spite of that, I started to see how a human female could be a boon when she brought picture books home for the young 'uns. They'd look at the pictures of elementals and see how humans read books. I was proud of 'em that they were interested and proud of Himself that he was introducing this human way of reading to the little 'uns. And when she made us tea and toast with honey and sat down to table with us, that was grand craic as well.

We've been lucky with the humans who've lived in the cottage with us. The early owners knew we were here and called it the 'faerie cottage'. Then, when Tanis lived here, the owners were holiday-makers who were only here for the weekends and summer, hence we had the cottage to ourselves. This is the way we want it. Because Himself is getting busier working with more elementals and humans too, it's nice to be alone in the cottage when company leaves.

After Tanis left, we weren't keen on the last couple who moved in full time. They didn't fit in with us or the vibrations of the place. They weren't settled and I have to say we made it a bit uncomfortable for them by pulling things off the table and unlocking the doors during the night to give them an oust. They started to think that the place was haunted. They even went to the village and spoke to the locals about Crumpaun being haunted and sure it was, haunted by us. We wanted them to think it. Normally, we try to get on and keep things easy-going with the humans we share our home with, but them, we wanted out. Thus, we gave 'em a little push. Even our goblin neighbors came to give more of a push and they're always willing to help out with something like that. Usually, we're having to hold them off but, in this case, we asked for their help. Goblins are the craftiest and smartest at figuring out how to get rid of a human, without killing him, of course.

Gradually, as me man's work became more well-known outside of Keel, human and elemental foreigners would trek to the cottage. I'd invite them in and make tea and then I'd go to the backroom. Yet I liked to overhear their conversations and was learning and changing from this. Also, after putting the young 'uns down in the evening, Himself and I would sit by the fire and he'd tell me about the road and I'd learn from him.

All this learning made me sorry about not having a little lass with whom to share it. The universe must have taken pity on me 'cos, about this time, young female leprechauns in the village started to visit me to hear the stories and then I didn't feel so alone. This was a slow process. Sure, I'm not moaning, as I chose to be in this cottage to be away from others. Leprechauns are solitary, not like trooping field faeries.

I'd love to tell you about me boys. Let's start with the youngest, as the eldest—Liam—will want his own word with you. It's past the time when he'll listen to his Ma about anything. The young 'un—Finn, we call him—is more like me. He's a bit of a dreamer; he's adventurous and likes to play the pipes, the bodrum—in fact, any musical instrument. Finn's a bit of a bard in the elemental community, which is an unusual craft for a leprechaun. Usually it would be an elf who would choose to be a bard but Finn's gone to study with the elves. He's got talent and the elves recognize it. The elves were pleased to accept him as an apprentice and this is another change in our world. Finn's been putting leprechaun stories and histories to song and he's keeping our traditions alive in that way. He can also play the fiddle and a small harp that he prefers to carry when he's traveling, so he can play music wherever he goes.

Finn's a bit of a wanderer like his Da and, even though you'd think of him as being a teenager, he's gone on trips recently with Himself. The elves encourage this as they think it's good for Finn to go out with his Da to hear stories from both elementals and humans on the road. In this way, he's part of the same group as his Da who wants to work with humans. Young Finn's got a foot in both camps. In our elemental world he'll be a bard and in the human camp, he'll bring the human and elemental stories together. We don't know where he'll settle ultimately and maybe he'll weave together these two paths. It takes a good weaver to keep old traditions alive whilst incorporating new changes. Finn's a weaver. I'm a weaver as well and a lot of the leprechaun and brownie woman in the village are weavers. So me son is weaving songs and we're proud of him.

I call me eldest son, Liam, the hooligan, and we need to use a firm hand to hold him on course. He wants nothing to do with the old ways and is always hanging out with the roughest elementals, the ones who are the most dissatisfied, including the rowdiest goblins and elves. Liam had a rough childhood as his Da was not around much and I was busy looking after the younger one. So the elder was on his own a great deal and we've got goblin neighbors his same age so that's why he hung around with the goblins. Sometimes I feel that he's learned more goblin than leprechaun ways.

I suppose I should turn it over to him to tell his own tale but, even as I'm calling him, he's in the pub taking a Guinness off the humans before they've a chance to drink it. Next, the humans will be complaining to the pub landlord about the bad quality of his beer and it's because me boy has already drunk the good essence out of it. So poor Marty in the pub will be blamed for this.

"I heard what you're saying Ma," said a young leprechaun, popping out of thin air. He had on a gaudy scarf tied around his neck, a large gold earring in one ear and was smoking a cigarette like a human. His eyes were hidden by sunglasses that continually changed shape and color and sparkled like a Christmas tree. His multi-colored Mohican haircut might have been the latest in leprechaun fashion, in a certain male age-group.

"In me own defense," Liam continued, "I'll have ye know that I make a tour of all the pubs round about and don't limit meself to the Annex. This is mighty considerate as I'm givin' the same reputation out to all."

"That may be, Liam," interjected Aine, "but your doin' yourself no favors carrying on like that and it's past time for you to settle on a craft like Finn's done."

"It doesn't do to compare me with Finn as he got his gift early. And you're not one to talk about taking the old path when you and Da cut your own trail," Liam retorted, turning red.

"You've got a point, son," replied Aine, conceding. "'Tis only I worry that you're never going to root yourself. Anyway, I'll say no more. Why don't you share your own tale? Sure I've no idea of some of the new-fangled things you're up to. I promise not to listen in, for I've me own work to get back to anyway."

The Eldest Son's Tale

I'd like to start by explaining what it's like growing up with Himself as me Da and, a while ago, he was elected the Grand, the leader of all leprechauns, which only made it worse. There's the rub! Following in me Da's footsteps is not possible. First, 'cos I'm nothing like him so I'm not interested in doing what he's doing. Second, 'cos he's so famous, not only among leprechauns but also among elementals in general, elementals wouldn't want to take me on as an apprentice. Yet, if I'm bein' honest, none of those traditional leprechaun jobs interest me anyway. So what am I supposed to do? I haven't a clue and that's not usual for elementals.

Normally, given me age, you'd think that I'd be getting some sort of sign by now, but I haven't, hence I'm putting in time until the light dawns. What I do know is that I'm neither a singer nor a bard like me younger brother. But I'm good at getting gold and lifting a purse.

Me goblin mates have taught me a lot of tricks, and from me troll friends I've learned to work out, so I'm fairly strong. Sometimes I lift up sheep just to make sure I can do it. I lift them up and put them down. Lift 'em up and put 'em down, but don't be telling me folks. I can tell you humans, which doesn't count. I quite like animals and I like to rescue young sheep that have been separated from their Mas. Leprechauns have always been around animals, but I've no mind to be a farmer. Farming is kind of going out of style now, but I wouldn't mind having some sheep and a coo as well. Sheep for the wool and coo for the milk. But I don't know if I'd want to look after them day in and out.

I often go to a neighboring village, where they don't know me well, and hire out. I've even been known to work for human farmers but they don't know I'm working for 'em. Then, don't be shocked, I take a bit of money after I've done it; 'tis only fair. It's hard to get gold these days but I can always get food. I like hanging around humans and working on farms. It doesn't suit long term but I learn a bit and I reckon all learning's good. I'm young and I'll figure out what I'm meant to do and, right now, I'm waiting for the right chance to come. I'm sort of in training but not to anyone or anything.

Me Ma's grand. I'm dead proud of her. She's very interesting and not boring like the other leprechaun Mas in the village. She's been very tolerant of Da and me and I don't want to let her down. Da and I don't get on well. It's like locking horns whenever we're in the same room, 'cos he'd like to be me boss and tell me what to do. He's used to being the boss, the Grand, and being the big man with others coming to see him asking for advice, but he's not me boss.

Lately, he's been learning to back off and let me go me own way. When he does this, I feel more comfortable and, occasionally, at night, if he's home, I'll stay in and sit there quiet-like and let Ma and Da talk between themselves. He knows I'm listening but I don't want to give meself away, so I sit there and stay neutral. His life and what he's doing is quite interesting but it's not for me. If he doesn't prod and probe to find out what I'm doing, we get on better. I think he knows that it isn't me time yet and, like him, I'll have to find me own way and 'tis taking a little longer than he'd hoped. But I'm not worried. What happens, happens. That's the way it is. That's what you've got to learn. You get up, day by day, and what happens, happens.

When I've had me fill of the country, I'm off to the city. There are leprechauns living in the cities and that's where you'll find the latest fashions. Right now, it's wearing formal tails over our arses and I'm ready to pick up some of these on me next jaunt. Often, we find an old house and squat in it and it's great craic to have some nightlife even if it's a bit crowded. 'Tis agreeable to visit the city but not to live there. I can travel to the city just by thinking of it; it's easy enough done, but the best craic is to go on me motorcycle as, with the wind blowin' in me hair, I pick up brilliant ideas of things to try out.

Also, it helps to talk to leprechauns in the city to get a feel for what they're doing. As for pubs, there's loads of them crying out for me to visit. You could say, I'm extending me options. We leprechauns love to meet in a pub and that's a good place to hear what humans are up to and some of us elementals are picking up new trades from them.

As you might know, leprechauns are famous in the elemental world as being good with gold and traditionally we're the bankers. These days, some are learning the human banking system so they can be even better at managing money. Recently, at least how elementals reckon time, many have become fascinated by the stock market and run bets on your human stocks to see which are going up and which down. Now, for sure, there's a game invented for leprechauns. We specialize in being able to talk you into or out of buying anything, hence we're amassing quite a bit of gold that way and some elementals are now having problems with gambling addictions. Elementals get addicted quite easy, but this gambling craze is causing quite a stir.

It's leading to a new craft—that of elemental counselling. We call it 'straightening you out' and it's to help folks who've lost their way. Some females who don't want to be midwives or matchmakers, 'cos the latter is going out of fashion, are apprenticing in this new trade. It might have appealed to me Ma, if she'd been born in me day, 'cos she's the kind of strong-willed female that likes to set a trend. And I've noticed that some of the younger females, who come to listen to Ma's teachings, are finding their way into the straightening-you-out craft.

Truth be told, you wouldn't find men going to a female for this or any other problem. For this reason, our men have started another way to straighten men out, which we learned off human males. We take yer man out of the city and back to nature. We get him off drink and into working with his hands. He goes from craft to craft and studies with men who are expert at their craft, with the result that he goes back to his roots. It doesn't mean that he'll stay with any of these crafts but, talking to the older men who are doing the crafts seems to stabilize yer man. Some Old Ones, our elders, make the rounds and talk to yer man as he's learning the new craft. Subtle-like... as leprechauns don't like to be told what to do.

We're having such success with this way of doing it that other elementals, goblins and the like are taking up the same approach and adapting our idea to their specific needs. For instance, if you're a trooping faerie, who's got into trouble with addictions, the Old Ones take him in hand and teach him singing and dancing and he's healed in that way. So, all in all, elementals are adapting well to the problems of modern life.

Another new craft taking off in cities has to do with creative advances in the building trade, which I guess you humans would call architecture. Admittedly, we pick up lots of ideas from humans but we veer in different directions. We're more into building with natural products, like wood and good earth, rather than using metal and plastic. And we're partial to making our buildings artistic and in harmony with nature and some of our young 'uns are making the buildings look like trees. These buildings have two, three, even four levels, and rooms extend out like the limbs of a tree, which go out to the sides with the little branches designed as play places for the little 'uns. The little 'uns love it up in the air. Quite a new thing for leprechauns to be off the ground, but good fun.

And 'tis not only leprechauns entering the building trade. Elves are best at the creative planning and envisioning beauty but they don't want to get their hands dirty. Trolls, on the other hand, are building down, down into the earth and, as many levels as we leprechauns have above ground, they've got below. And goblins are into building too. They do very well in the air and are especially interested in building the higher and more dangerous levels. They're even experimenting with making gardens in the higher branches so each home gets a garden. Some have even tried moving coos up there. Chickens are fine, and even a lamb, but 'twas a disaster when they tried coos.

Each clan usually builds for their own 'cos we've such different needs. However, lately, the goblins, leprechauns and trolls have experimented making complexes where they all could live happily together. Not totally successful… yet! There's been some mighty cave-ins as the hollowed-out dwellings the trolls make can't support the leprechaun and goblin structures on top. But it's only a matter of time till they master it and, if there's one thing—well, two things—you can say about trolls, it's that they're persistent and they're grand builders.

Me study, ye see, is moving about and studying the trends. I've a gift for seeing where elementals are going next and what they'll try out. Like me Da, I'm a bit of a leader in our community among the young 'uns. Not only here, but other places recognize me magnetism too. I've noticed over time that elementals listen to what I say and go where I want to go. Nice to be a leader but now I'm stepping back a bit till I figure out where I want to go next. Not that I'd be telling Da, but I've taken to sitting with some of the Old Ones to listen to their counsel. They're not much good on trends but they've got sage advice on leading. Furthermore, they've time for me and aren't pushing and I think they may have had a word to Da about this too.

As I said, 'tis very different that a leprechaun can't see his path before him and the Old Ones don't say much about it either. I figure there's something coming that's not been birthed so far but I'm getting a whiff of something in the breeze and it feels exciting. Could be to do with humans but not like me Da's interests. He thinks he's modern but I reckon he's old compared to me. Think I might need to do a bit of traveling to start with and hop into some other countries and survey the offerings.

Anyway, I've had me say. Ta for listening. Time to get back to me mates but, lastly, have a gander at me new disappearing trick that I learned off a banshee. Very rare that a banshee would share their gift, but I charmed it off her. To begin, I light up me ciggy and then I demonstrate the art of disappearing in a cloud of smoke in slow motion and complete with the sound effects of the banshee wail. Faaaarrrrrweeellllll!

Elemental and Human Differences

As the smoke was evaporating, Lloyd appeared with lots to say.

Ain't that the most awful yowl and this is how Liam spends his time instead of finding his path. I suppose he was telling you about the new-fangled inventions stupefying him. But I'm worn out worrying about him, so these days I'd rather focus on me own major interest, which is the differences between elementals and humans. I've a lot to say on the topic, 'cos I've studied humans for over a hundred years and have become quite an expert.

For instance, the subject of death. Humans are absolutely terrified of dying because they believe they'll no longer exist. That's caused by being glued to feeling you're unique and, if you don't mind me saying, that you're all alone.

Us elementals, on the other hand, know this is nonsense. Why? Because we can talk to others through our thoughts, not only to other elementals, but also animals and birds and crystals and all beings. Because of this and knowing their essence, we know they're alive and part of creation, even as we are. We're all part of the grand handiwork of the Creator. We believe in a Creator, as you humans claim to do; but, to most of you, 'tis theory and to us elementals, 'tis reality.

Another difference between you and us is that elementals know the other evolutions who are here on this planet. Sure 'tis easy to say we know about humans but how many of you know about us? Point made. Furthermore, elementals, unlike you, see other realms. We're living close by the angelic realm and so they come and go from our realm, even as they come and go from your realm, whether you see them or not. Long ago in Atlantis, humans spoke with the angels and other great beings who were helping your evolution and, at that time, humans could see and hear other realms much better than you do now. Your way of being then was more similar to the elemental way of being.

I don't want you to think that you've regressed, for it's not true. You are progressing and have developed your will and strong individual identity, your independence, whereas in Atlantis you were more in a dependent state. Therefore, you're further along on the path to becoming a conscious Creator. But you've got it wrong if you think you're alone and separate from others and all life.

Think of a flower on a fruit tree. Fruit trees have many flowers but not all of them turn into fruit. At the outset, all the flowers need to be pollinated and the bees or ants or the breeze do this. The flower depends on another for this to happen. After the flower is pollinated, it needs the energy of the sun and rain for moisture to mature the fruit. So, once again, the flower depends on others. It's the same for humans. You may have a good idea but you need others to support you in order to manifest your idea in the third-dimensional reality of your world. Nothing is created in isolation. The universe is interdependent and you will learn this in the Aquarian Age.

Elementals are evolving too. Like humans, we're moving from staying in our clans of goblins associating with goblins, leprechauns with leprechauns, and elves with elves, to speaking together and even being friends and working together to form a more inclusive community. And we're developing our will, which humans have made us do, in order to protect ourselves and our world.

We're helping you, too. How? Thousands of years ago, elementals who had developed the strongest will started to incarnate in human evolution. They are now hybrids—part elemental and part human. Because elementals are ahead of humans in the arts of dancing, painting, poetry, acting, singing, and making of crafts, these elemental hybrids have helped you to develop these arts and created more beauty in your human realm. The Creator hoped that, if humans had more beauty in their world, they'd want to go that way and not down the road of destruction.

Also, the group of elementals I work with who stay in the elemental realm, but still co-create with humans, are having an impact too. There's ever more elementals that want to partner with humans. Elementals have become aware of how their world is changing because of the new ideas that elementals, like me, are introducing. However, we learn from you as much as you learn from us. 'Tis fair to say that you are far ahead of elementals in psychology, philosophy, studying history—in fact, anything mental. We're learning to develop our mental bodies from humans. In this way, we become more objective and not so governed by our emotions.

The astral realm, where elementals live, is an emotional realm. But now, because we're beginning to develop our mental bodies, we're having more access to the causal realm of thoughts. Of course, we've always known that, if we have a thought of what we want to manifest, we only need to think it and we have it. Thoughts for elementals are spontaneous—kind of automatic. It's the same when we travel in space and time. We have a spontaneous thought and off we go. We have no doubt it will work, whereas humans have many doubts. You doubt that it's even possible. Humans have to think everything out with science and mathematics to prove it will work. Oh, I should add science and mathematics to the list of what you're teaching us. Remember that, will you?

Anyway, to live in the mental realm of thought, you've got to be able to hold onto an idea. For that, you need focus, concentration and will—not high on the list of elemental gifts, but high on the list of human gifts. Elementals are learning these qualities now. We were co-creators and friends before and we will work together in interdependence in the Aquarian Age. In fact, 'tis our destiny to be partners in creating beauty on the Earth.

Anyway, I guess you'd like to know how you can best meet and work with us. First off, there's certain times, like Beltane and All Hallows Eve, when the veil between your human and our elemental world thins and, if you're sensitive, you can glimpse our world. It used to be that if you were in a power spot, what you think of as a sacred site, such as Newgrange or Uisneah, you could cross to our world and the world of the ancestors. Nowadays, 'tis not so easy for you to cross, as your human realm is at a lower frequency than previously. Has to do with the way you've treated the Earth and other beings. Not good, not good at all.

Be that as it may, some can still cross and I'll point you in the direction of how to do it. It happens when you're dreaming and by developing your intuition and second sight. And how do you do that? It comes from meditating, not eating meat—especially pork and beef—and from working on erasing your negativity and in keeping your feelings pure and positive. A bit of laughter and humor also helps and that's a fact. Most humans need to lighten up and not be so serious. Enjoy the moment.

And did I mention that having an elemental friend strengthens your ability to come to our elemental realm and meet us? Your elemental friends want to work with you in so many areas, so choose. For instance, there's music, dance, film, creative writing, gardening, forest and environmental management. All these areas and more help humans come closer to our realm and the values of our people. If you're doing your best to create beauty and health for the Earth, we notice you. Even if you don't believe in us, such as scientists and other 'seeing is believing' types, who lean on proof using only their physical senses, we still help you. We do this by sending inspirations to point you in the right direction. You may call it 'a good guess' or 'a hunch' but it still comes from us.

Elementals exist in the smallest parts of matter—sub-atomic particles, you'd say—and we exist in the largest oceans. That's why we can help in pretty much any area that interests you humans. Yet earth elementals, such as the leprechauns, trolls, gnomes, goblins and elves, are most like humans, so it's easier for you to relate to and work with them. Sometimes you humans can see elementals, especially if we want you to, and mostly you see earth elementals like me.

You have a harder time seeing air elementals, which we call sylphs, or water elementals, which we call undines, or fire elementals, which we call salamanders. You might ask why that would be. 'Sure 'tis because those kinds of elementals have a higher frequency than earth elementals. Importantly, all elementals do much better when you appreciate and recognize us. Then we can work closely with you. We're looking for respect. We're intelligent beings who've worked with Spirit to build your world and you need to remember that, without us, you don't have a world or a life.

Which brings me to me next point. Each of you has a body elemental that builds your body. As you learn to work with your body elemental, you can heal yourself of all sorts of things you've created by fears and negative thoughts. I've not got time to cover that topic here, and Tanis has done a good job in her book *Good Morning Henry: An in-depth journey with the body intelligence*, so I'll leave it at that.

I just realized that I've been wandering. I was going to talk about the human fear of death and how you got it and now look where we've gone. It's proof that you humans are more focused than a leprechaun like me. Sure you'd start and end a topic on the same line but would it be as much fun? I never know where I'm going to end up when I start on a topic. I let it take me, whereas you like to take the topic. You see, I know that Spirit guides me thoughts of where it wants to go, so I don't resist it. You, on the other hand, often resist going where Spirit wants and, thereby, cause your own pain.

I'm thinking that the best way is combining both of our talents, which is to let Spirit take you but always keep your feet rooted on the ground. I must say I'm tolerably good at that. Probably most leprechauns are. In fact, better than elves. Elves are more daring than us and willing to try new things earlier, although their talent is a kind of soaring and falling. Leprechauns watch to see what works and what doesn't before we embark. We're expert at catching the elves when they fall and they take us up when they soar.

As I was saying a way back, before I side-tracked meself... humans, unlike elementals, fear death. Why? To start, we don't have illness and we've always been astounded that you create illness for yourself when it's not necessary. The fear of death creates illness. When you fear death, you're always looking for signs that you're dying. You focus on what's wrong with your body and, as you age, you find lots of things wrong. Cancer, heart problems, blindness, loss of hearing, not to mention things that go wrong below the waist! Elementals never think of these things. We love each stage in life—childhood, maturity, old age—and enjoy the gifts found in each stage. Our Old Ones aren't decrepit but are founts of wisdom garnered over centuries of living full lives.

To be sure, sometimes we get injuries if we behave like a right eejit, however 'tis elves who most often get injured experimenting with new things. They love adventure and get bored quicker than leprechauns and, in the olden days, they often stirred the pot by picking arguments and feuds with other clans. This could lead to arrows flying and deaths but that was all part of living the game of life. Death in war is not such a problem for elves any longer since they've many new things to occupy themselves.

For instance, they love to travel and sample the foods, music and entertainments of other kingdoms in the elemental world. They are connoisseurs of this. If they become bored, they can go somewhere else. Mind, as they age, even the novelty of change wears off, leaving a feeling of having done everything and felt everything. World-weary, you'd say. At such a time, a choice comes where they can either commit to learning something new, perhaps some new art form, or they fade.

Fadin' is how elementals die. When we're no longer drawn by life, we allow ourselves to fade. It's a kind of allowing. A human might see it as surrender but there is no fear of loss in it. Oh, there can be some nostalgia as we review our life. This can take years, decades even, and we can often linger in this stage to soak up the goodies in it as deeper allowing and fading occurs. Elementals are attuned to the natural rhythm of both the Earth and Spirit and know when the time for fadin' comes. We go into the ethers as our form dissolves. Humans fade too. Elementals can see it. But often you don't do it with grace and beauty, and fight every step of the way, thereby increasing your fear of death.

'Tis time to talk about morals—a topic humans seem to consider a great deal. Elementals are amoral, which I point out is vastly different from being immoral. 'Tis true we're beings of joy but we're neither unfeeling nor given to cruelty by nature. That said, what we consider to be acceptable behavior differs between various clans. Royal elves, for example, are concerned about presentation, how others perceive 'em. Are they beautiful? Noble? The best at the art they've chosen? Can they seduce the most desirable lover? Do you adore them? In this way, they are competitive but thoughts of having the most gold or being the smartest in philosophy, for instance, wouldn't enter their imagination.

Those things would perhaps be the desires of leprechauns, at least the one about gold. Also, leprechauns are proud of mastering their craft—very proud indeed—and also value being crafty and smart talkers. In fact, being able to outsmart a human with talk is one of our best games. Goblins, on the other hand, are what you'd call practical jokers. They're proud to trick and make fun of you and they're experts at holding up the mirror and pointing out what's amiss. They're not above a slight injury, such as tripping you on the lane so you fall in a puddle. Then again there are trolls who are proud of their physical strength. And if you're discussing the pride of field faeries, you'd best say they're the greatest in dance, music and play—all centered on their group and community.

Now that we've determined what various types of elementals are proud of and what they desire to be, you can imagine how they can be shamed. Our morals come into play when one of our own people steps outside what's expected of him. To me way of thinking, that's the same way it is for humans, isn't it? You've got standards for acceptable behavior and we've got ours. No right or wrong. Amoral versus moral. Phew!

I'll tell you another important difference between elementals and humans. Because elementals are telepathic, 'tis very difficult for one of us to hold a secret from the rest. Sure, maybe for a short time, but it will slip out. Humans, on the other hand, can get away with shameless behavior their entire short lives and no one finds 'em out. What do you think is the fairer way? I'd say, elementals knowing when one of ours shames himself is the best.

A royal elf shames himself if he takes what another does not willingly give. He lives by charm and, if charm doesn't work, the elf code is to depart with grace. Elves even use this code in seducing humans, which they've been known to do, but the human must come willingly to our realm. A crime to elves would be rape and abduction. A leprechaun, on the other hand, is shamed if he makes bad deals and gambles away his gold. Very bad, indeed. 'Tis even worse than not being able to excel at his craft.

Then there's goblins. Can you imagine what shames a goblin? It's when he goes too far with his tricks and seriously injures another. If you can laugh at what he did, that's fine, but sometimes a goblin may cause real injuries and then the community descends and puts him on probation and watches him closely. The reason for this law is that, if a goblin goes too far, the whole community of leprechauns, elves and others will want recompense. Goblins—who can blame 'em—prefer tricking an individual rather than taking on a community of angry trolls.

Speaking of trolls, they're shamed if they're a weakling. To prevent this happening, they do serious weight-lifting and muscle-building with rocks and trees, but sometimes brawn's not their gift. If that's the case, they may be good at finding veins of granite and crystal and what others want. That's a gift with trolls, which can save a weakling from shame. A crime for trolls would be to purposely kill one of their own, but that's a crime for all elementals. Same as with you humans. Universal law, that.

I'm trying to figure out if I've covered most of the differences between humans and elementals. Ummm... I've found another one. You humans need eight hours of beauty sleep per night to keep going. That's one-third of your entire short life. What a waste. That's a far cry from how elementals approach sleep. If we're doing heavy work, sure we need a rest after, but we don't usually rest as long as you.

When you sleep, you go to the astral world—the same place where you go after death, by the way. The human astral world is only a whisper away from our elemental astral world and some of you cross over into our realm and enjoy our world, at least for the time you're asleep. However, most of you forget your dreams and don't remember our time together. Most elementals leave you humans be if you come to our realm in your dream state. Why? Because you're a nuisance interrupting us from our business and always asking questions about this and that. Humans are dead curious. However, not all elementals leave you humans alone. The elves can spot a good-looking human and then she or he is fair game.

When elementals sleep, we go to higher astral realms where other evolutions exist, or even causal realms where thoughts come from. Most of us are as unconscious of beings in these higher realms as humans are unconscious when they come to the astral worlds where we, or other evolutions, live. Evolution continues in all realms and you don't die when the physical body dies. That's something humans and elementals have in common.

We're longer-lived than humans. An elf can live to a thousand years, although half or three-quarters of that amount is the most common. Leprechauns are long-lived, too. Field faeries, not so much, but trolls can match us, and then some. You could live longer in your physical world, if you kept to spiritual and natural laws. And 'tis natural for you to live longer in your astral and causal bodies, even as elementals do, when you're in the non-physical world. So, let's see, we've covered our differences with morals, death, lifespan, desires, shame, and how elementals are developing what humans are good at and how humans are developing what elementals are good at. I think that's it.

The Wake

I've already spoken about death and dying and you might have thought that you'd heard the end of it but I'd like to tell you a little tale. As you've summed up by now, elementals are that taken with human rituals that we often like to hang around 'em. For example, we like to celebrate your marriages for there's always great craic to be had there.

This is me lead up to telling the story of the grandest wake we've been at for a long time. The word went out that one of the human farmers in our community—Paddy, by name—was going to pass. He didn't have any of your wasting diseases, like cancer, but we could tell by looking at ole Paddy that his time was coming right soon. How did we know? We see a person's energy body—the etheric body—so we know if there's a blockage, or the color's off, or the energy's sinking. We can even see good things such as when someone's going to have a little 'un. And Paddy, poor Paddy, he'd a shadow round his heart, so we could tell his ticker was soon going to conk out. He was fading and losing his life force.

That's when Declan, me goblin friend, told me that the goblins had started taking bets on where and when Paddy would expire. "Would you like to get in on the action?" Declan asked. "There's some serious gold to be made and I know that always appeals to leprechauns."

"Have the bets been opened to leprechauns?" I asked, always suspicious of something too easy.

"Not exactly," he replied, "but I thought you'd like to hear from me first."

"And would there be a little something for you in this?" I asked, as I've a nose for how things were going.

"Only if you felt it fair," Declan answered, grinning mischievously. "I've a mind to put a little by to acquire me own cottage. I'm tired of squatting with me family when I'm not wandering the road recruiting goblins to work with humans. I've seen a right lass and think it's time."

"There's a surprise. What put those ideas in your head?

"Watching me leprechaun elder," he winked at me, "and seeing how happy he is with his mate."

"I'd like to hear more about the lass or do I need to spy on YOU?" I smiled, giving him a friendly thump on the shoulder.

"I'll be happy to ask for your advice, you bein' the expert, but not this moment. Now we'd best focus on betting. I've an idea that, if you add your gold to mine, we'll have a better position for bargaining."

Sure he had a good point. That Declan had a real leprechaun nature. "I'm in," says I, hoping that he'd as good a head for timing the farmer's demise.

"Me strategy is to stay in the middle of the options. What do ye say, man?"

"I'm for the middle if you know where the middle is."

"According to some of me goblin mates, he's already dead as that's the only way they'd get to claim on the gold they bet. Then others are saying he'll live another ten human years. I'm thinking of betting he'll be laying on a slab within ten days and I'm for putting a bit of money on each day until then. What do you reckon?"

"That's not far off, is it?" I said, "I'd best take another peek at his energy body to see if he's likely to drop so soon."

"Ah, sure, there's no need," replied Declan, trying to stop me from going to check. Him trying to stop me made me suspicious, so off I went to Paddy's field to find out if anything iffy was going on. Arriving, I caught sight of a bunch of goblins leaning on the poor man, whilst others were pulling them off. From their actions, it was easy to establish which ones had bet on the earlier and which ones on the later date for Paddy's dying.

When Declan saw 'em, he threw himself into the mix yelling, "Hold off. You'll foul the bets and no one will get a thing."

Grumbling, the leaners backed off and stared at Declan. "Fouling the bets is half the fun," complained an older goblin, cheered by his mates.

"Declan's got a point," said a young 'un, aligned to the pullers. "'Tis not really fair to take one minute from yer man's short life, is it?"

The young goblin received even more cheers and all settled down to the watching game but, luckily, not until Declan and I got in our bets. After that, there were watchers on both sides stopping any shenanigans before they got started.

Let's speed ahead to the day ole Paddy had his heart attack. It was one of the days near the end of the time that Declan and I had bet on. I was out the back stirring the poitín when Declan arrived. "What can I do for ye, Declan," I asked, stepping in front of the brew. No leprechaun would willingly share his poitín with drop-ins or there'd be nothin' left.

"I've an ethical dilemma about sending dying thoughts to Paddy so we can claim the gold," he said, attempting to keep his eyes off me poitín.

"'Tis not a dilemma for me," says I. "Me sympathy rests with the poor human."

"You're right, of course," replied Declan, "but sure that flies in the face of everything I've ever been taught by me family and community. It's known he's going to die anyway. Why not help him to a peaceful, quick death and collect the gold? That's the way I've been taught."

"That's fairly near to what I've been taught as well. Nonetheless, it's not the way I'm going now and I can see you're not going there either. You're complaining about what you already know you won't do."

"'Tis true," he laughed. "I'm that sorry for humans. I don't even want to trick 'em any more. Still, the gold would be handy."

Therefore, decision made, we waited for the day Paddy would die. Blessed be, on the last day of our bet, ole Paddy up and died and we collected, which brings me to the wake.

As Paddy was very traditional, the whole community of goblins, trolls and leprechauns were looking forward to the event. When the day came, me lass and I put on our best jackets. Our jackets weren't black like humans would wear to a wake, as I can't abide that color for me jacket, although I did have on me best black top hat in honor of ole Paddy.

I suppose I'd best inform you of how the Irish humans do a wake. To start with, you've got to have a dead person. Wakes usually take place at the dead person's home and, by the time we arrived, Paddy's wake was already underway. The curtains were closed, the mirrors covered, and the clock stopped. The family would have done this at the time of Paddy's departure and there he was lying in state on the dining-room table with candles at his feet and head and the window open for his soul to depart in peace.

Me and Aine had only been there a short while when a goblin party, dressed all in black, arrived. Behaving themselves, they walked single file around Paddy's dead body, murmuring about what a good ole farmer he'd been. So far, so good... until boredom set in. A young goblin blew out a candle at Paddy's feet, which set the others off chortling.

Paddy's daughter, Clare, thinking a breeze had done it, closed the window a crack and re-lit the candle. Clare had only just got herself seated when one of the young goblin's mates, winking at him, blew out a candle at Paddy's head. Up rises Clare to re-light it and to close the window a bit more. She'd only sat herself down again when the first goblin, not to be outdone, blew out two candles at Paddy's feet. 'Twas obvious the competition was on and the older goblins and leprechauns started to take sides on who was the better candle-blower and to nudge on their favorite.

That's when a third goblin leapt forward and, can you believe it, blew out all the candles in one breath. He was the obvious winner and received many claps on his back, even from me. It was well done and caused no problem and gave mighty craic. Even the humans, milling around and waiting to have their moment with Paddy, were smiling at these strange happenings. That included Clare who was beaming as she fastened the latch on the window. Irish wakes are usually filled with laughter and lots of banter, with many jokes and stories being told—all fueled by the drink.

No more fun to be had with the mourners, we set off to the kitchen where folks were gathered for the food and drink and to toast ole Paddy. Our timing was perfect for the next event. Paddy had been a regular at the local pub, and the publican, his hair slicked back and dressed in his Sunday best, was being helped by some young lads hoisting a keg of Guinness through the kitchen door. Seeing them struggling with the weight, some of us goblins and leprechauns ran to give them a hand. We can lighten your load, if we've a mind to, and, seeing the Guinness, we'd a mind too, alright.

"That lad on the right's a weakling," cried out Declan, running forward to support the sagging keg.

"Move over, Declan," says I, climbing under the keg. "'Tis a job for someone with more strength."

"If it's strength that's wanted," said one of our troll neighbors, grumbling from outside the door, "you'd both best move aside and let me do it."

With that, he picked up the entire keg and, hosting it onto his broad shoulders, started forward through the door.

"Amazing," said the publican, putting the keg down on the kitchen counter, "I'd have sworn the keg was heavier than this. Do you think it's the faeries?"

"Could be or we've a thirst for the Guinness," said the weakling lad, looking pleased with his new-found strength.

It's not uncommon for us elementals to hear such comments when we do a good turn. In some part of themselves, folks seem to know there's been outside help. More and more, they're crediting God or Mary rather than us and, although we'd prefer to be acknowledged, we're still happy they know it's help from other realms.

Yer man set to pouring drinks for those that wanted it—mostly the men but some women got in with their pints too. That's when one of Paddy's ole farmer mates, grabbing an empty pint and holding it out to be filled, spoke up. "In case the good folk are here, we'd best pour a pint for them too." He put down the brimming pint on the table beside the plate of sandwiches, and Paddy's wife, quick to see everything was going right, grabbed a few sandwiches off the plate and set them aside for us.

"This one's for the spirits," she said, as the others watched, "to make sure Paddy's welcomed where he's going. Sure he loved me bread and cheese."

"*Sláinte*," said yer man, raising his glass—a signal for the ole timers to salute us elementals and maybe for some modern humans to salute Mary or Jesus. That's when the drinking and toasting and eating got into full swing.

Wandering over to me, Declan declared, "I'm ready for a top-up. You?"

"Don't mind if I do," said I. "I see someone's brought poitín and I'd like a nip o' that to see if the human version can match mine."

Declan and I sauntered nonchalant like over to the poitín for we didn't want to draw too much attention. Our glasses full to the brim, I raised mine to him and declared, "Here's to you. You've got a good head on your shoulders. You'd have made a good leprechaun." That was the best compliment I could have given him.

"Now that you mention it, there's something I've been meaning to tell you," he answered, downing his poitín. "But before I do, I'd like another nip. 'Tis not half bad, sure."

I've got a bit more weight on me than poor Declan, him being a goblin and all, and I could tell by his slurring that he didn't need more poitín. Still, a friend is a friend and I wouldn't want him to drink alone. Not friendly, like. "I'll have a nip as well, then," said I, holding out the glass to be filled.

"'Tis a bit of a sensitive subject," said he, blushing crimson and knocking back his drink. "You need to promise you'll not laugh."

"That I can't promise but I'll give you a fair hearing," says I, wondering what could be so important and serious to a goblin, for there's nothing they love better than a good laugh.

"Remember you said I'd make a good leprechaun? Were you serious?"

Now I was curious. Where was he going with such a question? Nonetheless, he needed an answer. "'Tis true you've got many leprechaun virtues but maybe it's 'cos of hanging around me and me leprechaun mates, especially those that want you to spy for 'em when the women are discussing us for handfasting. That's when I came to know you better."

"That's the very topic I wish to discuss," said Declan, pouring another glass. "I've an eye on the mate I'd like...."

"Congratulations," I interrupted, raising me glass and saluting him.

"And," said he, looking at his feet, "she's a leprechaun lass." With those words, he keeled over.

That was the end of the wake for me. Digesting his tidings would have to wait. I signaled his goblin mates to help me lift Declan to his feet to carry him home.

Mixed Mating

Next morning, Declan showed up at me door looking poorly. Poitín's got a nasty kick the day after and any elemental can tell you that you're better off drinking your fill of Guinness than a lot of poitín.

"Last evening's a bit hazy," Declan admitted. "I should've known better than to drink the human's poitín as you don't feel yourself the day after. I woke up in me own bed but couldn't remember if we talked about anything special at Paddy's wake." With these words, he turned a fair shade of rose and I thought I'd let him hang there a minute.

"What kind of *special* are you meaning?" says I, tucking me thumbs under me armpits and smiling at him.

"Seems to me you were saying I'd make a good leprechaun," says he, smirking now.

"That seems to have slipped me mind. Maybe you'd best tell me about your *special* news again," says I, stretching out his misery.

"It started when one of your leprechaun mates asked me to do a spying job for a lass he was thinking of courting. As you know, I've built up quite a good reputation with leprechauns for assessing the quality of their lasses, but usually I'm consulted when they've already decided on the lass they want. In this case, I was the advance spy—let's say, counsellor, advice-giver… Have I mentioned, by the way, that I'm thinking of going into a new trade as a counsellor?"

"Get to the point, Declan," says I, wondering if he was ever going to get to the heart of his yarn.

"Look who's talking. After all the times I've waited for you to get to the point."

This issue he was circling must be mighty important to him or he wouldn't be stalling, hence I decided to be patient and consolatory—two virtues I've been cultivating.

"You've got a point. Take your time," says I. "Would you like some tea or shall we go down to the local?"

"Not the local," he answered, turning a pasty shade of green, "but perhaps a turn on the lane is just the thing." With that, he turned and strode out the door, his skinny legs churning so fast I could hardly keep up.

It was a soft day and the mist hung low and shrouded us, just how I like it. Declan was quiet and I wasn't going to be the first to speak for I could tell I'd an unfair advantage, him feeling unwell and all. Mates don't need to chat anyway and it wasn't until we had almost reached the deserted village that he opened the topic.

"The thing is I've me mind set on a leprechaun lass," he blurted out, eyes fixed on the ground.

'Twas as bad as bad could be. Leprechauns and goblins don't mix in handfasting, so he'd tumbled into a right mess. It was even a stretch that we'd become such good mates. Not usual, that. But mating? Bad. Neither community would like it. So what to say? I was speechless.

"No need to discuss the problems, as I'm well aware of 'em," stated Declan, kicking the stones on the path. "I came to you for your support and a solution. Can I count on ye?"

With those last words, he stared earnestly at me and held me fast with unblinking eyes. I was wriggling about with the pressure 'cos, if I agreed, it would be one more thing to add to the list of things I'd already done to rock me community. Leprechauns, on the whole, like a stable, predictable life and Declan's idea would not go down well. I did a quick assessment of the risks of me helping and did not like the odds. In spite of that, he was me mate and partner in hooking up elementals with humans. Also, he'd stood by me many a time when his goblin friends in Keel would have criticized me harshly.

"Sure of course I'm there for you, Declan," I declared. "Let's work out a plan. Have you any ideas? First, though, I'd best ask if the leprechaun lass has her mind set on you too."

He blushed deeper than before and quickened his pace, so I could hardly keep up.

"Let's sit on that rock over there," says I, breathing hard and heading into the field. He followed and plopped down beside me on a big slab of granite. I was the image of patience waiting for him to continue.

"I've had me eye on her for a while," says he. "She loves to wander by herself, just like your lass, and she's quite svelte for a leprechaun, which I think's attractive. Maybe too svelte for most of me leprechaun competition, which is good news."

"And has she given any indication that she's interested in you?" asks I, returning to me original question. There'd be no budging a leprechaun lass, stubborn as she'd be, if she was not interested.

"I've noticed her noticin' me," replies he, flushing again.

"And have you spoken to her?" asks I. It was hard work getting the facts.

"Not so you'd notice," answers Declan, looking downcast. "That's why I've come to see you. Thought you'd have a soft word with her, you being happily handfasted—or, better still, ask your lass to go. Takes tact. Very delicate. Because, if she doesn't want me, I'll not want it known that I was interested. If our elemental community in Keel found out I'd been rejected, they'd never let it go. What do you say?"

"Good idea, I'll ask Aine. She's good at this and many leprechaun lasses seek her out for advice, especially young 'uns who are developing modern ways. And, for sure, this idea of a goblin and a leprechaun handfasting is as modern as it gets."

"Right, then. Ask Aine to hint around to me intended and, if it seems me lass is hinting too, then make sure it comes out that I'm serious about handfasting not to… you know… take advantage…" Declan finished and, turning on his heels like a dervish, sped off home, leaving me to go at me own speed.

"Darlin'," says I, walking in me door. "Can I have a minute to discuss something Declan needs? And you've got to promise you'll not breathe a word to the other lasses or you'll break his pride." I paused to let her digest the importance of me request. "Here, have a seat," says I, gesturing her towards the stool, "and can I get you some tea?"

"What is it?" replies Aine, standing with her hands on her hips and a big grin creasing her lovely face. "Whenever you offer to get me tea, 'tis very suspicious."

I never knew that she knew that I did that. I'd have to find a new way to butter her up in future. Anyway, to the point. "Me darlin'," says I, "Declan's in a bit of a lather. He's focused on handfasting, which is a good thing as he sees how happy you and I are." I gave her me most winning smile.

"Aye," says she, keeping her hands on her hips. "Sooo…?"

Women, honestly. So difficult.

"Sooo…?" repeated Aine, giving me the *I'm waiting patiently* look.

"So, has any leprechaun lass given any indication that Declan was a good bet?" I asked, delicately.

"Could be," she answered, walking to the kitchen to put on the kettle for tea.

"And," says I, following her, "who might that be?"

"Who was Declan mentioning?" she answered, with the mischievous grin back on her lovely face.

"He didn't say," says I, kicking meself for not asking. "And who are you mentioning?" asked I, with me flattering smile in place again.

"I'd say Fiona might be interested. And, if she were, what were you wanting from me?" Me crafty lass knew full well she had the upper hand now.

I never would have called Fiona *svelte*. Also, she was on the far side of youth. But then a goblin's notion of beauty can be different from a leprechaun's. Surrendering to the inevitable, I asked, "Could you—all subtle-like—find if Fiona's serious about Declan?"

"That I could, dear. Would you like some tea?" said she, pouring boiling water into the teapot.

Aine, not stopping for tea, went off immediately for heavy hinting to Fiona. I was just finishing me tea when Aine returned and announced, "Declan's in luck. Fiona's interested."

"Well done," says I, giving her a big hug before heading off to Declan's.

"'Tis good news, Fiona's interested," says I, still wondering why he'd choose her from all the lovely leprechaun lasses.

"Who?" Declan asks, puzzled.

"Fiona, your intended," replies I, starting to get a bad feeling in me stomach.

"Eejit," screamed he, tearing his hair. "It's not Fiona I want but Roisín. How are you goin' to make it right?"

'Twas a right mess, for sure, but leprechauns are known for their fast thinking so I said, "Let's tell ole Oscar that Fiona has an interest in him. Because Oscar's a leprechaun, he's got that in his favor anyway. Also, he's been letting on that he's tired of his bachelor days and I heard tell Fiona's a fine cook. What do ye say? I'll see to him and send off Aine to tell Fiona that she meant to say Oscar not Declan. After all, both names sound similar, don't they? So 'tis easy to make a mistake. And, with Roisín, you'd best go yourself as I've done me bit."

Goblins are known for the gift to rebound and Declan took me suggestions in good stride. "You're right," says he, putting on his best jacket. "I'm off right now before you make another blunder. I'd best do me own courting. The news has most likely already spread around the neighborhood, so I've little to lose."

With them words, he was out the door. I hurried back home to ask Aine to make it right with Fiona, whilst I took on Oscar. Come to think of it, those two would make a good match. Oscar liked his food and had more than a little belly, not to mention that he was well into middle age. Aye, Fiona would match him nicely, with neither of 'em being the most desirable. Not nice to say but then the truth is the truth.

Aine was as keen as me to straighten out the trouble we'd created. Hence, we agreed to send each other secret messages through the ethers to make sure both of us were getting agreement. After all, we didn't want to create a bigger mess than we'd done already. Aine's a charming lass and was able to put such a positive spin on changing from handfasting with a goblin to a leprechaun that she'd an easy job of swinging Fiona to wanting Oscar. Meanwhile, with never a mention of the fiasco with Declan, I pointed out the advantages of Fiona to Oscar and he was keen on handfasting too.

Our good deed done for the day, Aine and I were relaxing in front of the hearth, congratulating ourselves, when Declan burst in. He was fair hopping around the room with a silly grin on his face.

"Tell us the news, lad?" says I, happy to see all had gone well.

Breathless, he began, "I arrived at Roisín's cottage at the same time as the matchmaker was being shown into the drawing room. What timing! Didn't I scurry up to the window to give a listen, only to hear Roisín's Ma say, "Roisín's not getting any younger so we'd best look at our options. Have you any likely men—I'm sure she meant leprechauns—for her."

"She's no great beauty, being so thin and all," answered the matchmaker, "but there are a few possible mates—the ole bachelor Oscar, for one. He approached me the other day about some possibilities but I didn't breathe a word until I'd your agreement."

"With them bargaining Roisín's life away, I hadn't a moment to lose. I crept around to Roisín's room and peeked in her window, only to see the poor lass waiting to hear what they'd decided for her. That's when I did something fair brave. I leapt through the window, missed me distance, and landed face down on her bed. Realizing immediately how that would look, I threw meself onto the floor, got down on me knees in front of her, pleading, "Please, dear Roisin, I'm no threat to you and want only your good. Will you hear me out?"

By then, she'd backed up against the far wall, but had, fortunately, not cried out. "Declan, what are you doin'?" she whispered. "You know it's not proper for any man to be in a maid's room. You must leave straight away."

"I will, dear Roisín," I got out. Me heart was throbbing to hear her say me name as, it not bein' proper, we'd never had a word with each other till that minute. "But please listen to me great hope. I've watched you from afar and think it possible you've been watching me and with a kind eye."

"It may be," says she, softly. "You've made a good reputation in our community with both leprechauns and goblins. You're hard to miss."

"Now that's the point exactly, dear Roisín," whispers I, quietly. "Working with Lloyd, me leprechaun friend, on getting humans and elementals together, I've come to know leprechaun ways very well indeed and to very much like leprechauns. I know it's not traditionally done for leprechauns and goblins to handfast but times are changing and I've me heart set on a beautiful leprechaun lass and I've come to ask your opinion of me choice."

Me face was burning up saying these words, but I knew plain talking was the only way. Time was short, with the matchmaker and her Ma in the next room busy arranging things not to me liking. Besides, by now she was blushing like a wild rose and hiding her smile behind her lovely hands, indicating that me next words would be welcome.

"I'd be pleased to hear of the beautiful lass who's taken your heart," she answered, her comely eyes twinkling.

"Why 'tis you, dear Roisín," says I, beaming. "I've noticed that you, like Aine, Lloyd's lass, like to try new things and thought you might be brave enough to take a goblin in handfasting. I can promise you an exciting life with a devoted mate. What do ye say? Shall we start a new way for leprechauns and goblins together?"

I was starting to ramble on with all the things I'd stored up to say to her, but leprechauns being more practical than goblins, she stopped me. "Declan," she said, "of course, me answer is 'Aye', so get up off yer knees and out the window before me Ma comes through the door. Then, get Aine and Lloyd to talk to me Ma and Da for you. Git, now, before the matchmaker and me Ma make a deal with a leprechaun for me. There's no time to waste."

"So here I am," says Declan, returning breathless at our door, "and you've got to go this very minute and speak to Roisín's Ma and Da."

"You're that moonstruck," says I, slapping him on the back and congratulating him. And off Aine and I went, giggling down the lane to the village, to bring Roisín's Ma and Da around to seeing the benefits of Declan and Roisín's handfasting. Aine and I were that pleased with ourselves that we talked about starting a new side-line of matchmaking for mixed mates. However, as we were, once again, probably going to incur the matchmaker's wrath by undercutting her business, we decided we'd best lie low on that promising business opportunity.

You're probably wondering what happened in the end. All was perfect and we ended up with two, not one, handfasting ceremonies. Sometimes mistakes turn out better than you could have planned. Furthermore, 'twas a bonus to get Declan settled with a nice leprechaun lass, for then I'd no longer be the only strange one in the village. He'd get his fair share of flak and, better still, it was one more step to moving things forward in a modern way.

Coronation of the Grand

Now I come to the high point of me story. By now, I'd made quite a reputation, not only among leprechauns and other elementals on Achill, but also among all elementals in Ireland. I was known for mixing modern with traditional ways to bring the best of elemental practices from all clans forward into the modern world. Also, I was proud to work internationally with elementals who either came to Keel to consult with me or wanted me to go to them. The intention of our new group never changed. We were focused on how humans and elementals could work together globally to create a healthy, sustainable Earth for our peoples as well as for all beings.

Now I'd like to tell you about the biggest event that a leprechaun can be involved in. Leprechauns don't have a high king like elves do. You could say we're run more like a democracy. This functions better for us as we like to express our opinions and are known to be independent. It's fair to say that we're proud and stubborn—not in a bad way, mind, but compromising is something we're learning from humans.

Having said that, we do have one tradition that has been handed down throughout the centuries. The greatest honor to be bestowed upon a leprechaun is the position known as the Grand. Usually, the Grand is elected in middle age and holds the station for many decades or even hundreds of years until he decides to retire and hand over his authority. This time had come for Manas, the current Grand, who'd done the job for a few centuries but had decided he wasn't up to helping us into the modern era. Leprechauns from around Ireland were chosen to represent their community to vote on who would be the new Grand. And, as I'd already established me reputation, I was chosen to represent Achill at the conclave.

Many leprechauns were gathered in Keel for me send-off. Each one had his opinions of who I should put forward as the new Grand. They'd been wagering on hot prospects and, for over a month, had been popping around Ireland getting a look at the possible candidates and they weren't above pressuring me for their choice.

One of Da's friends cornered me as I went to me shed. "I think Rian's the best bet," says he, "'cos he's from Tara and the sacred Boyne Valley where our people originally settled. Location. Location. What do you think, lad?"

I didn't have to respond as, just then, Colm came around the corner and started in. "Nonsense. We're over full of that ole family stuff. I'm for a new man. Diarmuid from Ulster in the north has me vote. He's had to deal with human technology much longer than here on Achill, hence we'd best elect him. You'd agree, sure, wouldn't you, lad?"

At this point, Da arrived and saw his mates badgering me. "Leave him be! Have you not realized that he's a fine candidate himself for the job and that you might be eating your words soon?"

That's me Da, proud of his own, as he should be, and didn't his mates take the hint, clap me on the back and wish me luck.

'Tis true that you're never valued in your own village, even if you're celebrated afar.

To escape more opinions, I bid them farewell and fled inside me cottage, followed quickly by Da. That's when Ma appeared and set to.

"We think you've got a good chance at being named the Grand," began Ma. "Have ye thought about what you'll say if you're nominated?"

"I've said the very thing to him," agreed Aine. "What with our two young 'uns to look after, I'm not sure he's got time."

"It would put more on you," said Ma, seeing things from a woman's view.

That's when Da volunteered his opinion. "But, if he was the Grand, it would be good for the boys and the whole community. Think of the trade we'd get. All our crafts would be in demand and I could even open a shop, which I've been thinking of, selling to tourists. It would be the first of its kind. Very modern. I could serve me famous poitín, which would definitely encourage sales."

Aine, Ma and Da stared at me to see which way I was leaning. What a fix! There was no way I could meet everyone's needs. The good news is that all the hullabaloo had prodded me into contemplating what I wanted and how it would likely affect family and friends, as well as the country. That was a worthwhile exercise and I came out of it sure that I'd run as a candidate. Being the Grand might be a sacrifice for me family but it would be a chance to get more elementals interested in working with humans. These thoughts went through me mind in no time, leaving me the task of making it good with Aine.

"If I became the Grand," I said, "I understand how it would benefit the community. However, as I'd be away a lot, it would be hardest on you and the little 'uns. So I think you should have the final say." This was one of the hardest speeches I'd made to Aine in our time together. What if she said, *Don't do it.* What would I decide then?

Aine gave me 'the look'. Every man knows 'the look'. In a flash, she saw everything that would happen. Me going... her and the boys alone. I could see that she was weighing this vision with how much she also knew I'd want the position and the good I could do. That's when Ma stepped in.

"I'll be happy to help with the little 'uns. I'd like some more time with 'em and, if your Da's going to start a tourist shop, I might as well put me time into something as well."

"Well," says Aine, smiling at Ma and then me. "'Tis settled, then. We'll be fine here. Off you go and good luck to you. You'll make a fine Grand. Sure we all know that!"

I went to the conclave with a light heart, knowing I'd the support of me family. A man can't have too much of that, now, can he? And who was the first man I ran into but Shamus, me leprechaun friend from the Midlands who I'd not seen for donkey's years. Since last I'd seen him, he'd got a bit heavy in the middle but his playful grin announced he was still up to having good craic.

"Shamus," says I, giving his shoulder a friendly punch. "What a fine occasion that we're both here to elect a new Grand—hopefully one who'll be partial to us elementals working with humans."

"Indeed," says he, smiling broadly. "And do ye think it could be one of us? Wouldn't that be the best?"

"Sure 'tis exactly what I was thinking," I replied to me ole mate, "and I've a plan."

"When have you *not* got a plan," say he. "Let's hear it."

"Before we get to the plan, do you want to be the Grand? If you do, the plan won't work."

"I'd love to be the Grand but I've five young lasses at home and their Ma would have me head if I accepted. However, if it were meant to be, I think she'd bend to the wishes of the conclave. I wouldn't mind if you nudged the conclave a bit towards thinking of me. I take it that Aine's got your back at home, you lucky lad, so get on with it. What's the plan?"

"To begin with, we've got to get ourselves elected as candidates, so I'll put you forward if you'll stand for me."

"Done. But there's Diarmuid and Rian still wanting the job. What do we do about them, since those are the two we'd have to get by?"

"Exactly. That's why I need your help. I can't alienate any of the followers of either of them if I'm to come out on top. I've got to come across as having the best qualities of them both. This means you've got to undermine both Diarmuid and Rian and get their followers thinking of me."

"I see," answered Shamus, crossing his arms across his broad chest. "Sweet smelling roses for you and thorns for me. And how's that to me advantage?"

"I've given that very question a lot of thought and there's two main reasons you'd want to help get me elected. First, I'm the closest to your own views on where we have to take elementals if we want to survive this modern world. Rian's got the noble blood so he'll always have the ole guard voting for him; therefore, we need to demonstrate that the traditional leprechaun way won't work in the modern world. We can't stay in our homes making shoes and poitín and philosophizing in the pubs. Then there's Diarmuid who, to his credit, is wanting change. But he's a bully who'd try to lord it over elves and goblins and, you know as well as I do, that this will split elementals into factions. Then our energy would be wasted on elemental infighting instead of implementing ways to work with humans to help the Earth."

"You've got a strong opening point but what's the second one?" he asked, his arms still crossed.

Every fool knows that, friend or no friend, you've got to sweeten the deal if you want full cooperation. Shamus needed something personal for himself. Shamus and I were that knackered trotting around Ireland getting elementals interested in partnering with humans that it was only natural we needed some hope of a good time to enjoy ourselves.

Pushing back me shoulders and holding his gaze, I dangled the carrot. "I think we've got to extend the influence of elementals beyond Ireland. I'm going to need to travel globally to work with elemental communities to interest them in our vision. I'd need a stand-in for when I'm abroad and you're the man for the job. You can think of it as a part-time job so your lass and family won't feel you're missing.'"

He uncrossed his arms immediately and pinned me in a hug. "That's a grand plan and you can count me in," said he, squeezing so tight I struggled for breath. "I'll get on it, directly. No sense waiting until we're candidates to promote ourselves. I'm off to sing your praises and put a dent in Rian's admirers. You go to Diarmuid's supporters and be the calm voice of reason to show how, if Diarmuid gets elected, it will lead to infighting among elementals. I'm sure most haven't even thought of that."

Accordingly, that's the plan we followed and by the time I nominated Shamus and he nominated me, it was clear that one of us would get elected the Grand. This called for our second negotiation.

"Shamus," said I, after I got him off by himself, "we've done a good job of dealing with Rian and Diarmuid, but now we've another problem. You've been so visible, what if you get elected or do you want that?"

"Not at all," says he, "I'm sticking to the plan to be your stand-in but you've not thought far enough ahead. If I don't look like a good solid stand-in, our conclave will never agree to it. You're always starting new ideas and not all of these men are fans of yours for doing this. I've got to come a close second and decline near the end when I state sadly that it would be too much traveling, with me young family. Hesitating to accept the nomination because of me family will go down well at home and that way I'll also get the traditional leprechauns on me side. That's when you offer a compromise plan of you being the international ambassador and me being the local lad… which I'll just have to graciously accept."

Wasn't he the crafty fella, that he'd one-upped me and cut himself a larger slice of the pie than what we'd originally agreed on. But didn't he deserve it and I'd a feeling we'd work well together, so I said, "Good plan and who gets called the Grand?"

"You do," says he, all magnanimous, "except when I'm in residence." With his last words, he collapsed laughing.

That's how I became the Grand… most of the time. And that's how me mate Shamus and I got the perfect deal for us both. But I suppose you want to hear about the coronation, so I'll not keep you waiting. After all, that's the high point of me story. Did I mention that we were at Uisneah? Maybe you've never heard of it—which would be your loss, and one I'll happily remedy.

Uisneah is located in the center of Ireland—the navel of our sacred isle—and the veil between the worlds is thin there. The Tuatha de Danann, who are the ancestors of elementals, lived in Uisneah with their queen, Eiru, which gave rise to Ireland's name. That's why it's sacred to us. Often, if an elemental has lost his way, he'll go on pilgrimage to Uisneah to find it. At Uisneah, we can speak to the ancestors of all the clans, of the elves, leprechauns, goblins, trolls. When there's a sacred ceremony to be had, we trek to Uisneah and, from time beyond time, we've held the election of the Grand on that hill in order to receive the blessing of the ancestors.

The conclave had been going on for many days by the time it was decided I'd be the Grand. We'd time to catch up on each man's life and how things were where each one lived. From the stories, it was clear that the traditional leprechaun way was no longer possible. They knew I'd take them in the direction that, like it or not, leprechauns and all elementals would have to travel to find a place in the modern world.

The common themes were that trees and forests were being cut down and small farms were being lost to large businesses. The farmers who, for centuries, had respected the land and elementals were being forced off from lack of money. It was evident that, if elementals didn't find new, younger supporters who valued elementals and the land, our race, like our ancestors, would be vanquished to other realms and our energies lost to the Earth. This would lead to devastation for the Earth and all beings.

None liked this vision at the conclave and Shamus and I had the most experience working with humans in partnership devoted to Earth healing. Thus, it was agreed that the time had come to find allies globally among elementals and humans. Strength no longer could be found in isolation but only in community. These lessons tasted bitter in many mouths because leprechauns don't change easily, especially when we're not sure of what good we'll get by changing.

Shamus, as good as his word, had thrown his vote behind me with the understanding that he'd be the stand-in when I was touring the world talking to elementals to convince them to implement our vision. Leprechauns have a reputation for having a good head on our shoulders for making practical plans and delivering on them. We're also good at convincing others of our plans and the leprechauns in our conclave were proud to think that Irish leprechauns would be international elemental leaders.

Now, back to the coronation ceremony. It was held in the open, 'cos we're beings of the natural world and thus want the elements of earth, air, fire and water to witness our sacred ceremonies. The leprechaun delegates made two lines facing each other to create an aisle down which the ole Grand would take his final walk. Manas was a strong leader and had held the leprechauns together for a few centuries. Although he had white in his beard and was no longer a man in his prime, he was anything but decrepit. However, he'd been fairly traditional and it was clear, with him calling the election himself, that he didn't feel up to the task of taking us into the modern age. That he wasn't so proud to hold onto power when it didn't serve the community proved his good character.

The leprechauns had donned their best clothes. Some were attired in more traditional browns and greens, and others, wanting to prove how modern they were, wore purple or red jackets with black dress trousers. One, stressing his 'hipness', even wore rainbow-colored shoes that me boy Liam would have coveted. Some of the older ones leaned on canes and the younger ones fidgeted at how long it took for their elders to get in line. But, on two themes, all conformed. Each wore a top hat unique to his home community, plus a shamrock, the symbol of our leprechaun clan, on his chest.

As Manas began his slow walk down the aisle, he was dressed in our traditional garb of green jacket and brown trousers, and his black shoes shone with silver buckles. Across his shoulders, he wore a stole covered in green shamrocks, each one embroidered with the names of the villages and towns he represented. Symbolizing his office, he carried a golden staff with a large crystal on top.

Walking erect, he nodded and greeted each leprechaun in turn, even those who hadn't been his greatest supporters. I witnessed him closely and was picking up lessons to apply to me own time as the Grand. When he got to me, he winked, showing me that, even after two centuries of carrying the load, he still had his humor at all the proceedings. He walked to the head of the aisle and turned to face us.

"Friends," Manas began, "it's been me privilege to represent you for these last centuries and an honor that you chose me to be the Grand. I've done me best to hold our community together and to celebrate and promote your many gifts." As he said these last words, he smiled at the older, more traditional leprechauns and they smiled back and cheered him as their own.

Next, he turned to the younger, more modern-leaning ones and continued. "At the same time, I've not been blind or deaf to the words for change and have done me best to accommodate needed changes in our communities." As he spoke, he smiled at the modern delegates and they cheered him too. What a good politician, I was thinking and was reminded of how important it was to have agreement from leprechauns with diverse ideas.

"But the time has come," he carried on, "to implement changes introduced by those who have been on the front lines of change. It's their ideas that must root if we leprechauns and all elementals are to make a successful transition into the modern world. These changes have been introduced to our community by both Lloyd and Shamus and 'tis not easy for me to say which one would be the best choice as the new Grand. Lucky for me," he added, smiling and turning his head to take in all the leprechauns, "you've freed me from making the choice."

Looking at me, Manas continued, "I now call Lloyd to step forward and for you to greet him as the new Grand." With that, he gestured for me to stand to his right and to turn and face the conclave.

I was on the point of starting me acceptance speech, when Manas added: "And Shamus," said he, gesturing to him to come forward and stand on his left, "as the leprechaun conclave has decided, you'll be the stand-in Grand when Lloyd is away."

Everyone cheered at Manas's words and, once again, I was learning the way from me elder. He had much to teach me and I'd ask him for advice at the next opportunity. Shamus was better at making friends and smoothing feathers than me, whereas—no sense being falsely humble—I was best at thinking a new idea and doing it. Together, we'd make a good team.

Manas gestured for me to face him. When I did, he removed the stole from his shoulders and draped it on mine. Then he took his golden staff and with the words, "I welcome you as the new Grand," bonked me on the head with the crystal and handed me the staff. Dazed, me speech evaporated and I entered a place where I saw the ancestors in higher realms lined up accepting me in their midst. Manas gazed at me with understanding and I realized that he, and probably every Grand, had had the same experience but had kept it secret.

With heart open and feeling the honor that had been bestowed on me, I turned to Shamus and said, "And I welcome you, Shamus, as the stand-in Grand when I'm abroad or cannot attend to the many duties here for our community." With those words, I bonked him on the head with the crystal and saw that he, like me, had gone to be welcomed by the ancestors too.

That's how our leprechaun community got two Grands instead of one. To this day, Shamus and I work together both in Ireland and around the world to assist elementals who want to partner with humans to heal the Earth. Therein ends me story.

Slán agus beannacht, as we say on the Emerald Isle—farewell and blessings to you.

Part 2

Faerie History from Local Humans

I have recorded what was said to me by local Keel residents about both the faeries and Lloyd's Crumpaun Cottage. However, to protect their privacy, I use only the first names of those still living. The names of the deceased are accurate.

The current owners of Crumpaun Cottage bought it in 1992. When I was visiting Keel and gathering local history to write the book for my leprechaun friend, I phoned them.

"Hello," I began, "my name is Tanis Helliwell and I lived in the cottage in 1985. I was hoping I could visit you tomorrow and speak to you of the cottage's history."

"We've read your book about living with a leprechaun in our cottage, so we know who you are," replied Anne, a smile in her voice.

"Yes, that's me," I acknowledged, less nervous now to speak about their cottage being 'haunted' by leprechauns.

"Don't come too early."

To which I responded, "How about 10:30?"

"Ah, that's too early."

"How about 11:30?"

"That would be fine," I replied. This gives you an idea of how early is *early* on the west coast of Ireland.

Since I lived there, the current owners had renovated the cottage inside and out. The plaster had been removed from the outside walls and the original stone exposed. When I lived in the cottage, the roof was slate, and I had seen on an earlier visit that the slate had been replaced by thatch. Therefore, I was surprised that the thatched roof had, once again, been replaced by slate. Eamon saw me looking at the roof and commented, "We had it thatched in 1996 to restore it to what it would have been originally and, at that time, we were told it would last 50 years. However, the crows picked at the straw and the thatch was too heavy and wet, so we had to replace it with slate again in 2014. Look here at the initials and date on the stone we uncovered when we removed the plaster in the renovation: MG and 1749, so we think that is when the cottage was built."

"I understand you don't live here full time, is that right?" I asked, wanting to confirm what the leprechaun had told me.

"We live in Dublin and come for holidays but our daughter Maeve lived here for a while with her man. They loved it as they're surfers and they surf here."

"If the cottage is 250 years old, can you tell me more about the former owners?" I asked.

"The young couple who had it before us were only here a short time. His name was Murt— short for Matthew, I think—and she was French. The council owned the cottage and gave them a mortgage but I think they didn't pay and that's how we got it. For more information, you'd best ask Gerry, who was the postman for many years."

Saying goodbye, I headed down the lane to Gerry's house. He had been the postman when I lived in the cottage in 1985 and he recognized me right away. His wife, Bernie, short for Bernadette, showed me in and gestured to a seat. Gerry had some trouble walking and took the seat opposite me. However, his mind, even at 84, was keen in remembrance.

"I'm tracing the history of Crumpaun Cottage," I said to him, "and wondered if you knew what the initials MG stood for on the corner stone on the cottage?"

"I'd say it could mean Michael or Martin Gallagher. Gallagher's daughter Eliza was the aunt of Lily Barrett, who became a White when she married. Lily's daughter owns the guest house where you're staying.

"I remember her mother from when I lived at Crumpaun Cottage," I commented. "She told me that her family had once owned it and that they'd called it the faerie cottage. Have you ever heard tell of the cottage being haunted?"

"That I have," Gerry answered. "Deliah was the name of one of the people who lived in the cottage and Deliah had a nephew, Steven, who sometimes stayed in the cottage. He and I went to school together and Steven would speak of the good people, the *daoine maithe*, living there. When Deliah died, the cottage was vacant a good long time before the Davidsons [not their real name] bought it, and they had it when you were there. Then, when the Davidsons sold it, I heard about how the leprechauns had become upset with the next people who lived in the cottage and tried to make them leave. Anyway, that's about all I can tell you."

"Thanks for your time and it's been grand seeing you again," I said. Bidding Gerry and his wife goodbye, I walked down the lane to town and back to Tom's workshop, the very place where this story began.

Tom was around back and, seeing me, he was quick to ask, "Have you been finding out the local history for your book?"

"Yes, I've discovered many things about Crumpaun Cottage and its owners and even some stories about the little people."

"My wife Anna and I have had experiences and, if you'd like to come in, we're happy to tell you."

I didn't need to be asked twice. "I'd love that," I answered at once.

Tom, signaling me to follow and crossing the yard to his house, went through the door and into the kitchen. Anna turned as we entered and Tom introduced me. "This lady's interested in the faeries. She used to live in Crumpaun Cottage and I thought you'd like to speak with her."

"That would be fine," replied Anna. Smiling and pointing to a chair, she said, "Sit down and have some tea."

Sometime later, as we were finishing our tea, Anna asked, "Do you want to know more about Crumpaun?"

"I'd like that. I'm curious to know if you heard anything about the couple who bought the cottage after the Davidsons sold it," I replied.

"Well, I was in O'Malley's when the couple came in and I overheard them ask Maureen, who worked in the shop, if she knew of a cottage to buy. Maureen said, 'Why don't you try the White's cottage.' This was Lily White's cottage and she owned the guest house where you're staying."

"Excuse me," I interrupted, confused, "but I thought the Davidsons owned the cottage at that time."

"That they did," replied Anna, "but we still call it the Whites' cottage. Anyway, the couple only lasted a little while and later came asking Maureen, 'Why did you recommend a haunted cottage? Even the front door opens in the middle of the night'."

"Maureen said, 'I told you if you bought it that you'd need some holy water.'"

The couple said, according to Anna, that they'd brought in a clairvoyant to try to pick up something but she didn't find anything.

Anna continued, "The couple were put out and didn't last long. After that, the cottage was bought by the current owners and their daughter's man surfed with our son. Sometimes he'd say that there must be kids playing pranks on him as he'd lock his car at night and it would be open in the morning."

"Kids or the faeries, wouldn't you say?" I smiled at Anna, while Tom listened in.

"Ah, definitely. There's a bog behind Crumpaun called *fear bréige*, meaning *scarecrow* or *fake man* in Irish. My father, Martin Lavelle, said he got tripped up by the faeries in the bog and broke a few ribs."

"Why do you think that happened?" I asked.

"I couldn't say but at the time there were no street lights in Keel, as they only came in the 70s, and he'd been given a new pair of binoculars that he was carrying."

"Do you mean the faeries were mad at your father for taking on modern ways?" I inquired.

"Could be," Anna replied. "The traditions have been dying out since the 70s. Both my grandmother and brother could see and hear something three days before it would happen. We'd only talk about this in the family and keep quiet to others. I think people have lost this ability, down through the generations."

"It's the same in my family," I shared with Anna. "My mother and brother, like me, have this gift of second sight but only in later years did they speak of this, even to me."

"I've had a similar experience in this same house," shared Tom. "One night, I was awakened and could hear Anna's father's voice in the next room but her father was dead. I went to his room and saw a human-like being, who was not Martin, sitting on Martin's bed, which went down with its weight. It was misty but had a shape and I looked three times and then said, 'I see you' and it disappeared.

Anna got up at that moment, crossed the room, and brought back a piece of wood, which she handed to me. "It's a piece of faerie wood from Clare (county Clare) and it has healing powers. It's from a healer who brought it to Keel to heal a young man from depression for his grannie had been letter bombed in the north of Ireland. Here, smell it."

"It smells like the outdoors," I said, smelling the wood. "What kind of tree do you think it's from?"

"Probably a hawthorn. They're special to the faeries," replied Anna. "And even today we use such things for healing."

"Is it only in Keel," I asked, "or do you hear mention of faeries in other parts of Ireland?"

Anna was quick to answer. "Even on the news, lately, there's a story of a young couple in Clare who were told by their father not to build a house on a *sidhe grogans*. That's a piece of bog that is raised like the dome of a church and is special to the good people. But the couple built it and, as it was on the leprechaun's path, both the front and back doors would be open in the mornings."

"That's the same story we heard about the couple in the Crumpaun Cottage," I replied.

"That it is," Anna replied, nodding wisely.

It seemed that she and Tom had shared all they knew of the faeries, especially those in Keel, so I gathered my notes together and said, "I appreciate your time in sharing so many stories about local history and now I'd best get my notes typed up to record all I've learned. Thanks, Tom, for lending me the computer, so I could get it all down."

Acknowledgements

Firstly, I wish to thank Simon Goede who kindly and patiently listens to me reading several drafts to discover, each time, where to put those blessed comas to capture the Irish lilt. Mentioning 'Irish lilt', I wish to gratefully acknowledge Olga Sheean who edited the book perfectly according to Irish idiom.

Then came the cover and design. Nita Kay Alvarez discovered and developed the perfect cover that Lloyd, my leprechaun friend, would accept and Melany Hallam completed the book design and layout in an inviting and cozy fashion. Thanks to you both.

Lastly, I thank Lloyd's fans who have embraced him as an old friend and who have a continuing curiosity about his life. It is you who have inspired Lloyd's autobiography.

Further Reading on Nature Spirits

Arrowsmith, Nancy (with George Moorse), *A Field Guide to the Little People*, McMillan, London, 1977.

Evans-Wentz, WY, *The Fairy Faith in Celtic Countries* (1911), University Books, New York, 1977.

Froud, Brian (with Abu Lee), *Faeries*, Harry Abrams Inc., New York, 1978.

Huygen (ill. Rien Poortvliet) *Gnomes*, Harry Abrams Inc., New York, 1977.

Helliwell, Tanis, *Summer with the Leprechauns: The authorized edition*, Wayshower Enterprises, 2011.

Helliwell, Tanis, *Pilgrimage with the Leprechauns: a true story of a mystical tour of Ireland*, Wayshower Enterprises, 2010, 2020.

Helliwell, Tanis, *Hybrids: So you think you are human*, Wayshower Enterprises, 2015.

Helliwell, Tanis, *The High Beings of Hawaii: Encounters with mystical ancestors*, 2019.

Hodson, Geoffrey, *Faeries at Work and Play*, Theosophical Publishing House, Wheaton, IL, 1982.

Gregory, Lady, *Visions and Beliefs in the West of Ireland* (1920), Gerrards Cross, Snythe, 1970.

MacLean, Dorothy, *To Hear the Angels Sing*, Lorian Press, 1980.

MacNamara, Niall, (ill. Wayne Anderson), *Leprechaun Companion*, Pavillon Books, London, 1999.

MacManus, Diamuid, *Irish Earth Folk*, The Devin-Adair Company, New York, 1988.

Papenfus, Stan, *Paddy's Chin*, Life Cycle Centre, Ireland, 2003.

Pogacnik, Marko, *Nature Spirits & Elemental Beings*, Findhorn Press, Forres, Scotland, 2004.

Roads, Michael J., *Journey into Nature*, HJ Kramer Inc., Tiburon, CA,1990.

Rose, Carol, *Spirits, Fairies, Leprechauns, and Goblins*, Norton, New York, 1996.

Small Wright, Machelle, *Behaving as if God in all Life Mattered*, Perelandra, Warrenton, VA, 1987.

Tompkins, Peter, *The Secret Life of Nature*, HarperCollins, New York, 1997.

Von Gilder, Dora, *Fairies*, Quest Books, Wheaton, IL, 1994.

Yeats, WB, *Fairy and the Folk Tales of the Irish Peasantry (1888) and Irish Fairy Tales (1892)*, reprinted SmithMark Publ., New York, 1996.

About the Author

TANIS HELLIWELL has given transformation and healing workshops internationally for over 30 years. She is a leading-edge psychotherapist, well known for working to heal physical, emotional and mental traumas and patterns. Tanis teaches her techniques internationally to groups of psychiatrists, physicians, psychotherapists as well as to the general public.

In addition to her psychotherapy practice and workshops, she worked consecutively for 30 years as a consultant to businesses, universities and government to create healthy organizations, and to help people develop their personal and professional potential. She was a faculty member of the Banff Centre for Leadership for over 20 years and numbered IBM, and many medical, social service and environmental agencies among her clients.

Tanis Helliwell is a sought-after keynote speaker whose insightful awareness is applied in a variety of disciplines. She has presented at conferences also featuring Rupert Sheldrake, Bruce Lipton, Matthew Fox, Barbara Marx Hubbard, Gregg Braden, Fritjof Capra and Jean Houston. These conferences include The Science and Consciousness Conference in Albuquerque, The World Future Society in Washington, DC and Spirituality in Business conferences in Boston, Toronto, Vancouver and Mexico. She has also presented at Findhorn, Hollyhock, ARE Edgar Cayce, Alice Bailey and Anthroposophical events.

In 2000, she founded the International Institute for Transformation (IIT), which offers programs to assist individuals in becoming conscious creators to work with the spiritual laws that govern our world. Her online, in person, and self-study courses include Transform Yourself, Co-creating with Nature Spirits to Heal the Earth, Ancestor and Family Healing, and Self-Healing with the Body Elemental.

She is the author of the classic *Summer with the Leprechauns as well as Pilgrimage with the Leprechauns, Manifest Your Soul's Purpose, Decoding Your Destiny, Hybrids, The High Beings of Hawaii, Embraced by Love* and *Good Morning Henry*. Her books have been translated into eight languages.

She is committed to helping individuals to develop right relationships with themselves, others and the Earth.

Tanis Helliwell
1766 Hollingsworth Rd,
Powell River, BC, Canada V8A 0M4

tanis@tanishelliwell.com | www.tanishelliwell.com
www.facebook.com/Tanis.Helliwell

Books & Resources
by Tanis Helliwell

BOOKS:

- Good Morning Henry: an in-depth journey with the body intelligence
- High Beings of Hawaii: encounters with mystical ancestors
- Hybrids: so you think you are human
- Summer with the Leprechauns: a true story
- Pilgrimage with the Leprechauns: a true story of a mystical tour of Ireland
- Decoding Your Destiny: keys to humanity's spiritual transformation
- Manifest Your Soul's Purpose
- Embraced by Love: Poems

Videos:

1. Elementals and Nature Spirits, https://www.amazon.com/dp/B01B6O1YLM/
2. Hybrids: So you think you are human, https://www.amazon.com/dp/B01AVB30SG/

MP3s available on our website:

Series A—The Self-Healing Series: Talk and Visualization
1. The Body Elemental/Healing with the Body Elemental
2. Rise of the Unconscious/Your Basic Goodness
3. Reawakening Ancestral Memory/Through the Veil Between the Worlds

Series B—Spiritual Transformation Collection: Talk and Visualization
1. The Celtic Mysteries/Quest for the Holy Grail
2. The Egyptian Mysteries/Initiation in the Pyramid of Giza
3. The Greek Mysteries/Your Male and Female Archetypes
4. The Christian Mysteries/Jesus' Life: A Story of Initiation
5. Address from the Earth/Manifesting Peace on Earth

Series C—Personal Growth Collection: Two Visualizations
1. Path of Your Life/Your Favorite Place
2. Eliminating Negativity/Purpose of Your Life
3. Linking Up World Servers/Healing the Earth

Made in the USA
Las Vegas, NV
17 March 2023

69242673R00094